DINOSAURS
AND PREHISTORIC PREDATORS

Dinosaurs and Prehistoric Predators, May 2011. First Printing. Published by Silver Dragon Books, Inc., 433 Caredean Drive, Ste. C, Horsham, Pennsylvania 19044. Silver Dragon Books and its logos are ® and © 2010 Silver Dragon Books, Inc. All Rights Reserved.

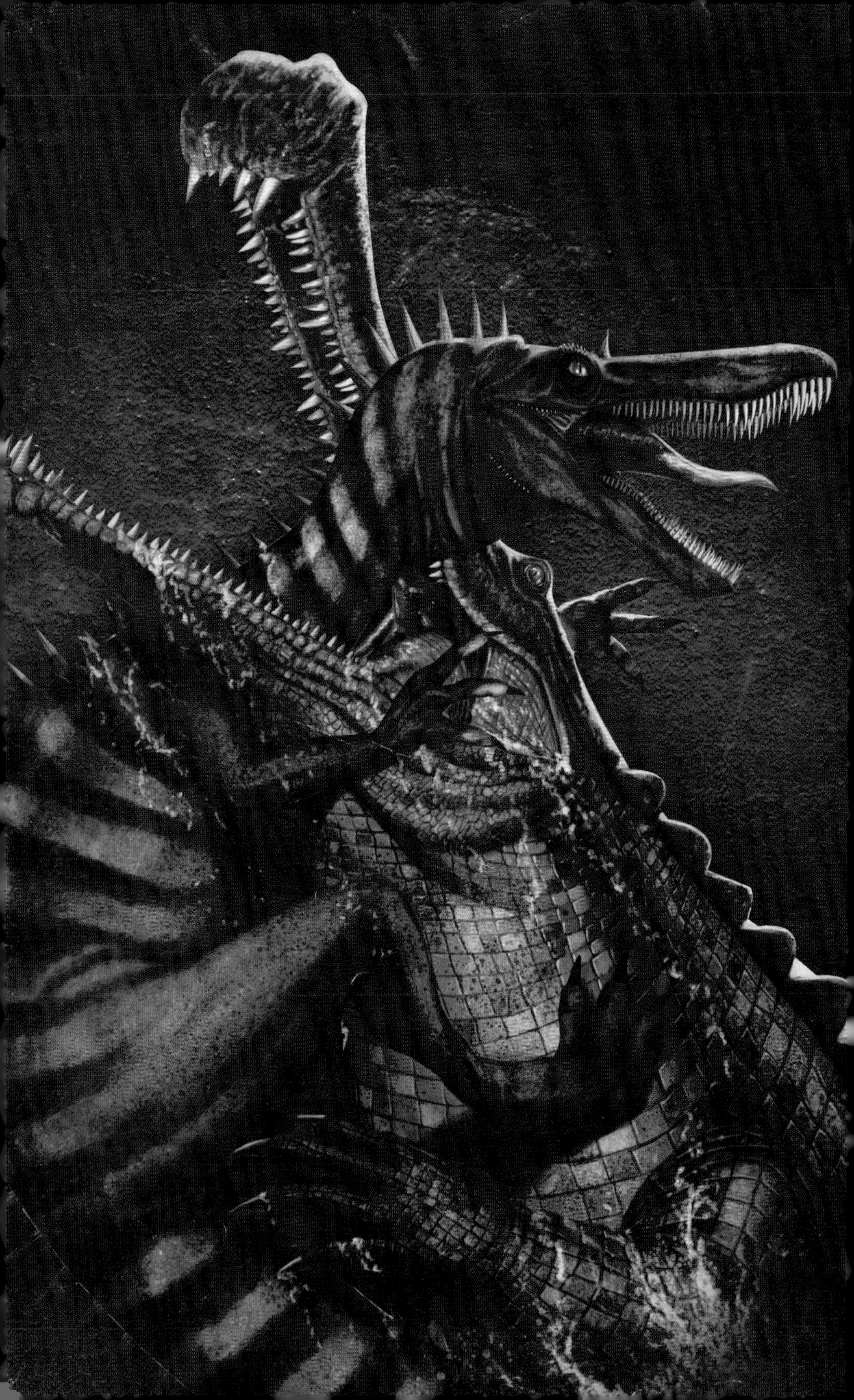

WRITTEN BY
JOE BRUSHA, NEO EDMUND, ROBERT GREENBERGER
PAUL KUPPERBERG, AARON ROSENBERG, JIM SPIVEY

ARTWORK BY
CAIO CACAU, DSAGAR FORNIES, ALEJANDRO GERMANICO
CHRISTOPHER GUGLIOTTI, GORDON PURCELL, ROBIN RIGGS
RAE ROCHELLE, ANTHONY SPAY, ALESSANDRO VENTURA

COLORS BY
CAIO CACAU, MAX FLAN, MARCIO FREIRE
MARCELO MACEDO, ALEX SIQUEIRA

LETTERS BY
JIM CAMPBELL

PRODUCTION AND DESIGN BY
CHRISTOPHER COTE

COVER BY
MANNY CARRASCO, STEAMBOT STUDIOS

PUBLISHER
JOE BRUSHA

MANAGING EDITOR
JENNIFER BERMEL

EDITOR
ROBERT GREENBERGER

SPECIAL THANKS TO
ELIZABETH BAKACS, GRANT MCALLISTER
SARA SHAFFER, EDU ALPUENTE, KLEBS JUNIOR

PUBLISHED BY
SILVER DRAGON BOOKS
433 CAREDEAN DRIVE, STE. C
HORSHAM, PA 19044
WWW.SILVERDRAGONBOOKS.COM

FIRST PRINTING
978-0-9327507-4-2

Discovery CHANNEL

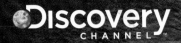

DINOSAURS

FINALLY, THE ANKYLOSAURUS DECIDED IT HAD HAD **ENOUGH.**

FIRST, IT USED ITS **HORNS** TO MAKE GIGANOTOSAURUS BACK OFF.

A **SECOND** TAP GAVE ANKYLOSAURUS ROOM TO **MOVE.**

OW IT HAD THE **SPACE** TO JSE ITS MOST **EFFECTIVE** DEFENSIVE WEAPON...

THE SMALLER DINOSAUR SWUNG ITS ARMOR-PLATED CLUB TAIL.

THE BLOW FROM THE ANKLOSAURUS' TAIL PACKED ONE HECK OF A *PUNCH.*

FWAM

AND
PREHISTORIC PREDATORS

TRIASSIC PERIOD

251 TO 200 MILLION YEARS AGO

THE PERMIAN PERIOD WAS A FERTILE TIME FOR EARLY-LIFE ON EARTH. AT THE TIME, LAND WAS ONE MASSIVE CONTINENT CALLED PANGAEA, HOWEVER, A MASS EXTINCTION EVENT, CALLED THE GREAT DYING, OCCURED, WIPING OUT MORE THAN 90% OF LIFE ON THE YOUNG PLANET. ITS CAUSE REMAINS A SUBJECT OF SPECULATION.

THE DINOSAURS ROSE TO PROMINENCE IN THE WAKE OF THE EXTINCTION, AS PANGAEA MOVED NORTHWARD. GREAT SEA CREATURES, SWAM THE OCEANS AND POWERFUL CREATURES ROAMED THE WARM LAND. THE FIRST TRUE DINOSAURS APPEARED AROUND 230 MILLION YEARS AGO. IT IS ALSO THE ERA WHEN THE FIRST MAMMAL LIFEFORMS EMERGED.

JURASSIC PERIOD

200 TO 145 MILLION YEARS AGO

THE CREATURES WE KNOW AS DINOSAURS REIGNED SUPREME DURING THE JURASSIC PERIOD. THEY GREW IN SIZE AND DEVELOPED VARIOUS WAYS OF PROTECTING THEMSELVES OR OBTAINING THEIR PREY. PANGAEA ALSO BEGAN TO SPLIT APART, SEPERATING THE LIFEFORMS.

CRETACEOUS PERIOD

145 TO 65 MILLION YEARS AGO

THE CRETACEOUS PERIOD IS THE MOST EXPLOSIVE PERIOD AS DINOSAUR, ANIMAL, AND FISH DIVERSITY GREW IN SCOPE. PANGEA'S COMPONENT PARTS SPLIT FURTHER, A HARBINGER OF MORE DRAMATIC CHANGES THAT WOULD EVENTUALLY DOOM THE DINOSAURS. THE DINOSAURS BEGAN TO EVOLVE INTO SPECIES THAT NOT ONLY ATE PLANTS BUT MEAT.

A E A

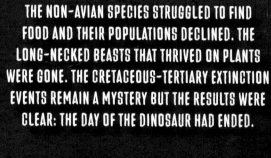

THE NON-AVIAN SPECIES STRUGGLED TO FIND FOOD AND THEIR POPULATIONS DECLINED. THE LONG-NECKED BEASTS THAT THRIVED ON PLANTS WERE GONE. THE CRETACEOUS-TERTIARY EXTINCTION EVENTS REMAIN A MYSTERY BUT THE RESULTS WERE CLEAR: THE DAY OF THE DINOSAUR HAD ENDED.

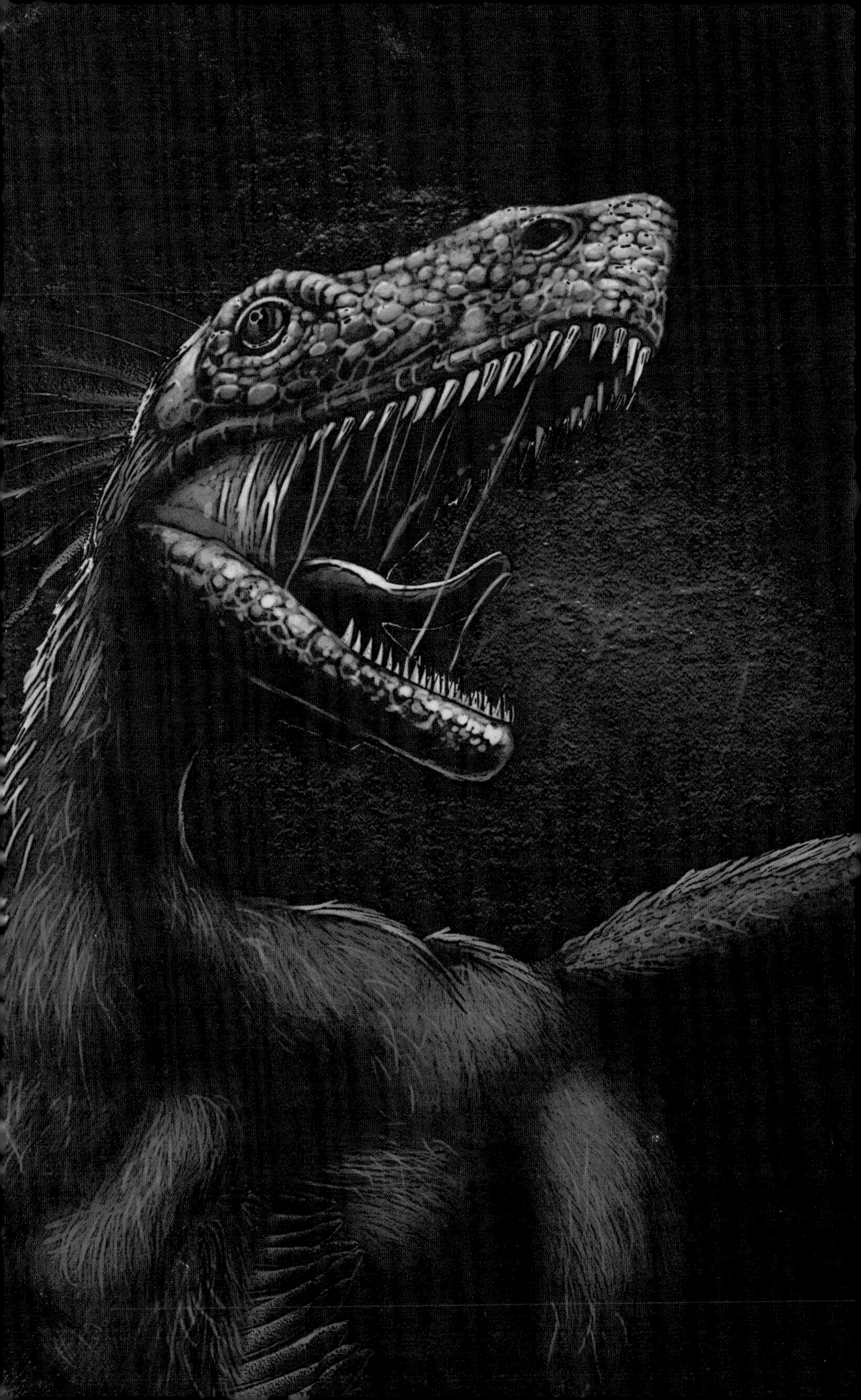

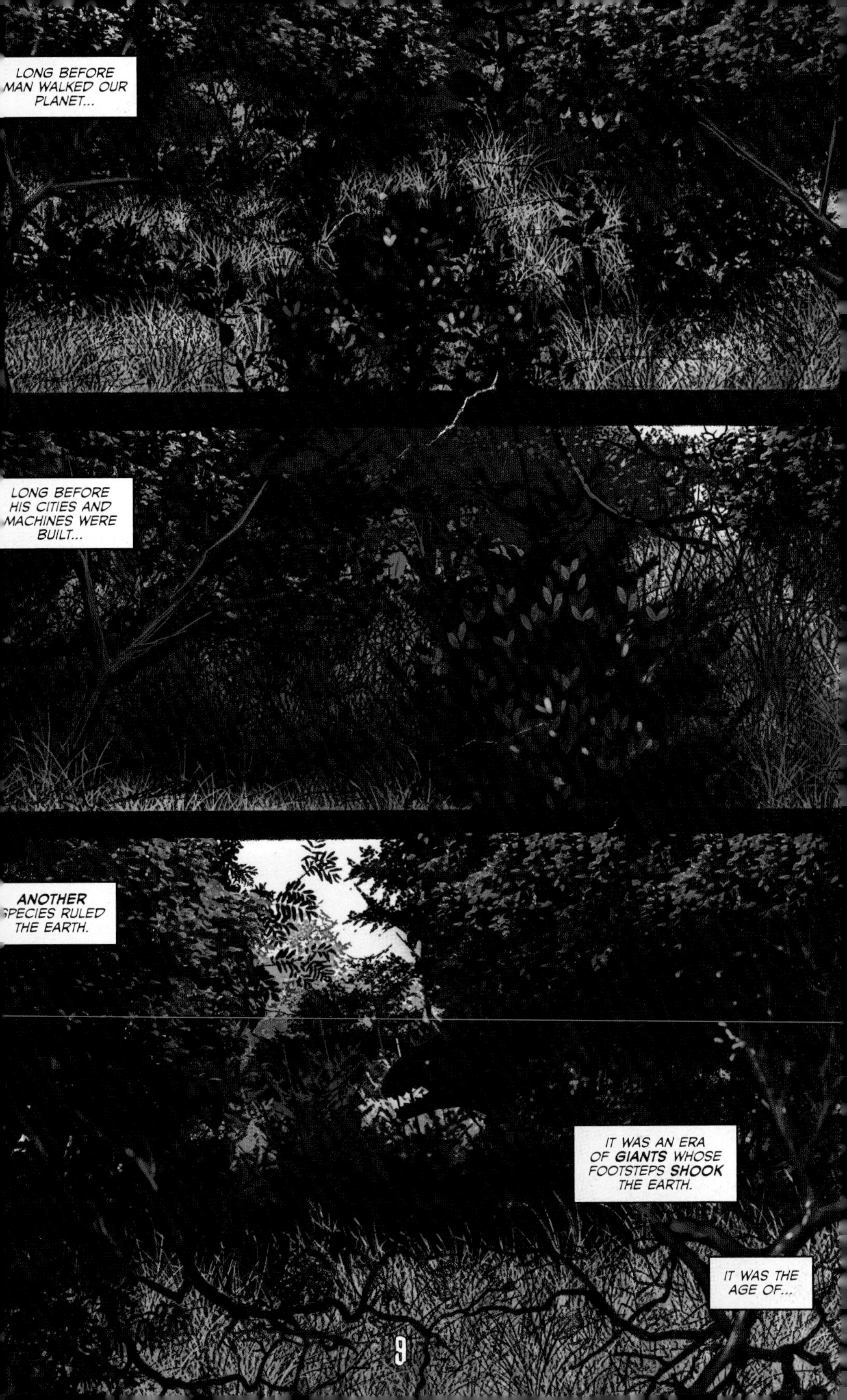
LONG BEFORE MAN WALKED OUR PLANET...
LONG BEFORE HIS CITIES AND MACHINES WERE BUILT...
ANOTHER SPECIES RULED THE EARTH.
IT WAS AN ERA OF **GIANTS** WHOSE FOOTSTEPS **SHOOK** THE EARTH.
IT WAS THE AGE OF...

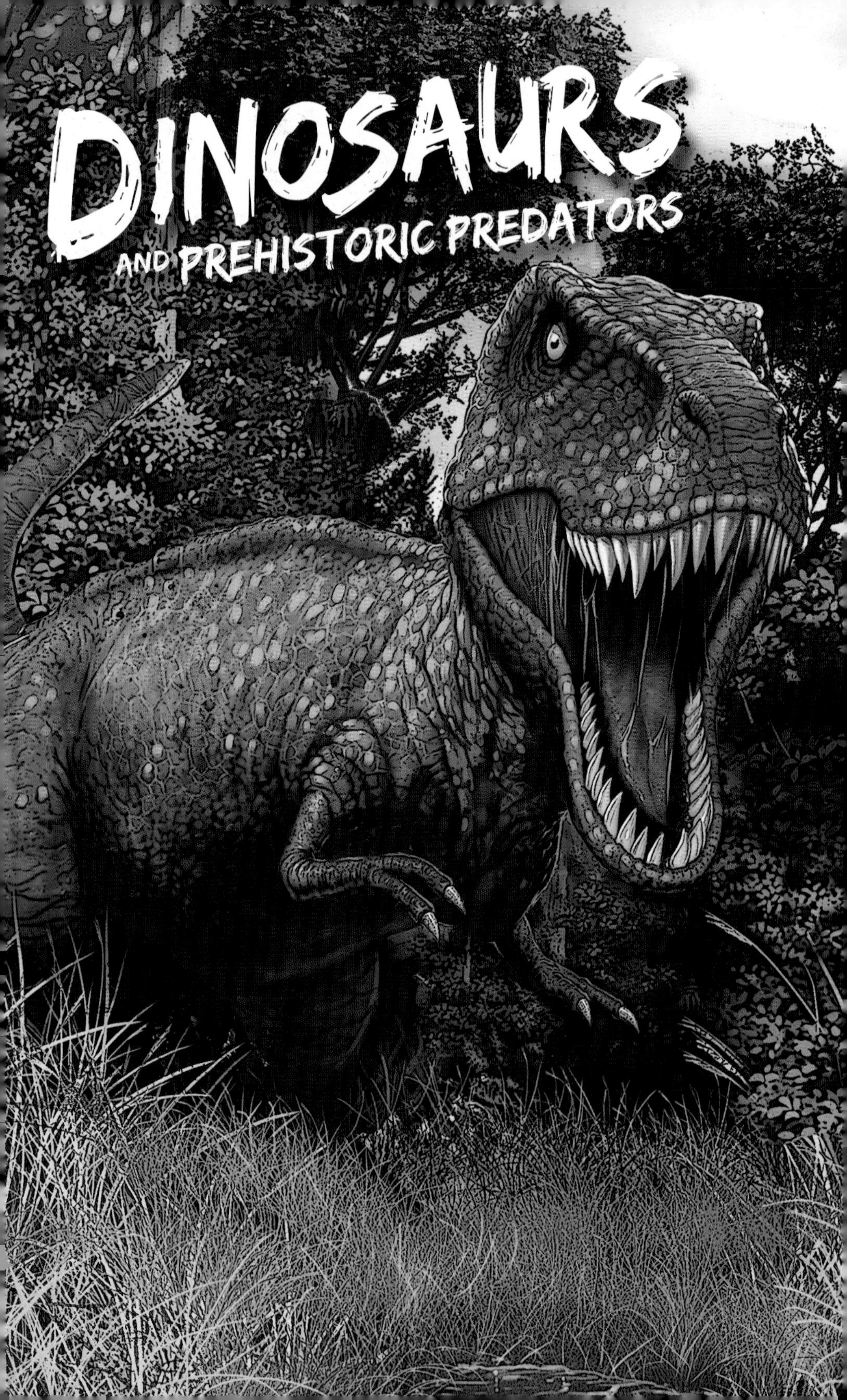
DINOSAURS
AND PREHISTORIC PREDATORS

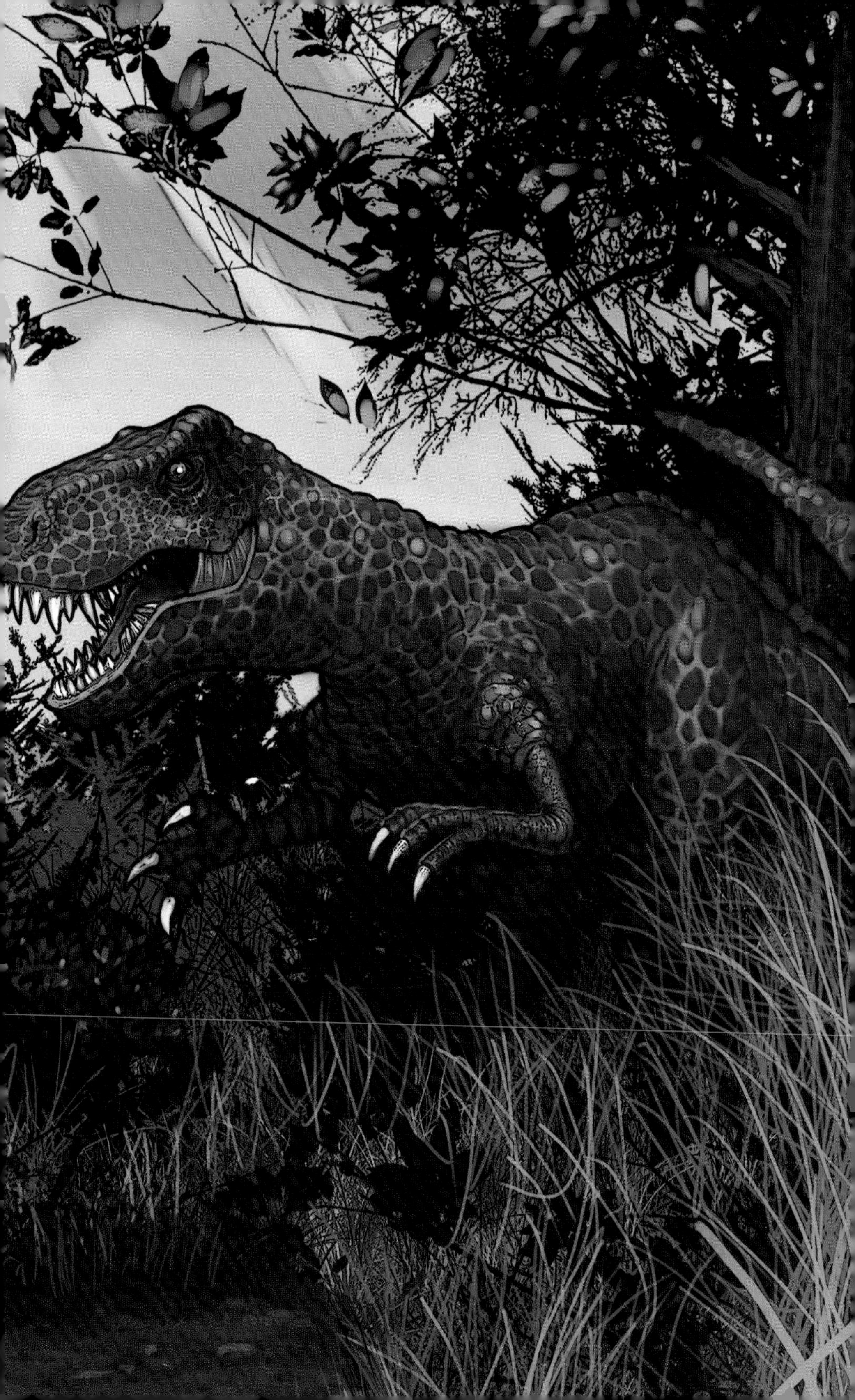

THE NAME DINOSAUR MEANS TERRIBLE LIZARD.

THESE GIANT REPTILES LIVED UP TO THEIR NAME.

NOTHING LIKE THEM HAS BEEN SEEN ON EARTH BEFORE OR SINCE THEY BECAME EXTINCT.

WE DON'T KNOW FOR SURE HOW THEY BECAME EXTINCT.

MANY SCIENTISTS THINK THAT A HUGE METEORITE STRUCK THE EARTH ABOUT 65 MILLION YEARS AGO.

THE IMPACT WOULD HAVE CAUSED A CLOUD OF DUST AND DEBRIS TO BLOCK OUT THE SUN FOR MONTHS LEADING TO THE STARVATION OF MOST SPECIES ON THE PLANET AT THAT TIME.

BUT THAT'S JUST ONE OF SEVERAL THEORIES THAT ARE CURRENTLY BEING EXPLORED.

WHAT WE **DO** KNOW IS THAT THERE WERE **HUNDREDS** OF SPECIES OF DINOSAURS THAT LIVED DURING THE **MESOZOIC ERA.**

SOME OF THE BIGGEST WERE **HERBIVORES,** EATING ONLY PLANT MATTER.

OTHERS WERE THE GREATEST **PREDATORS** THAT HAVE EVER WALKED THE EARTH.

THIS GRAPHIC NOVEL LOOKS AT THE DINOSAURS THAT AT ONE TIME WERE THE MOST **FEARED** AND **FEROCIOUS** ANIMALS ON THE PLANET.

ALLOSAURUS

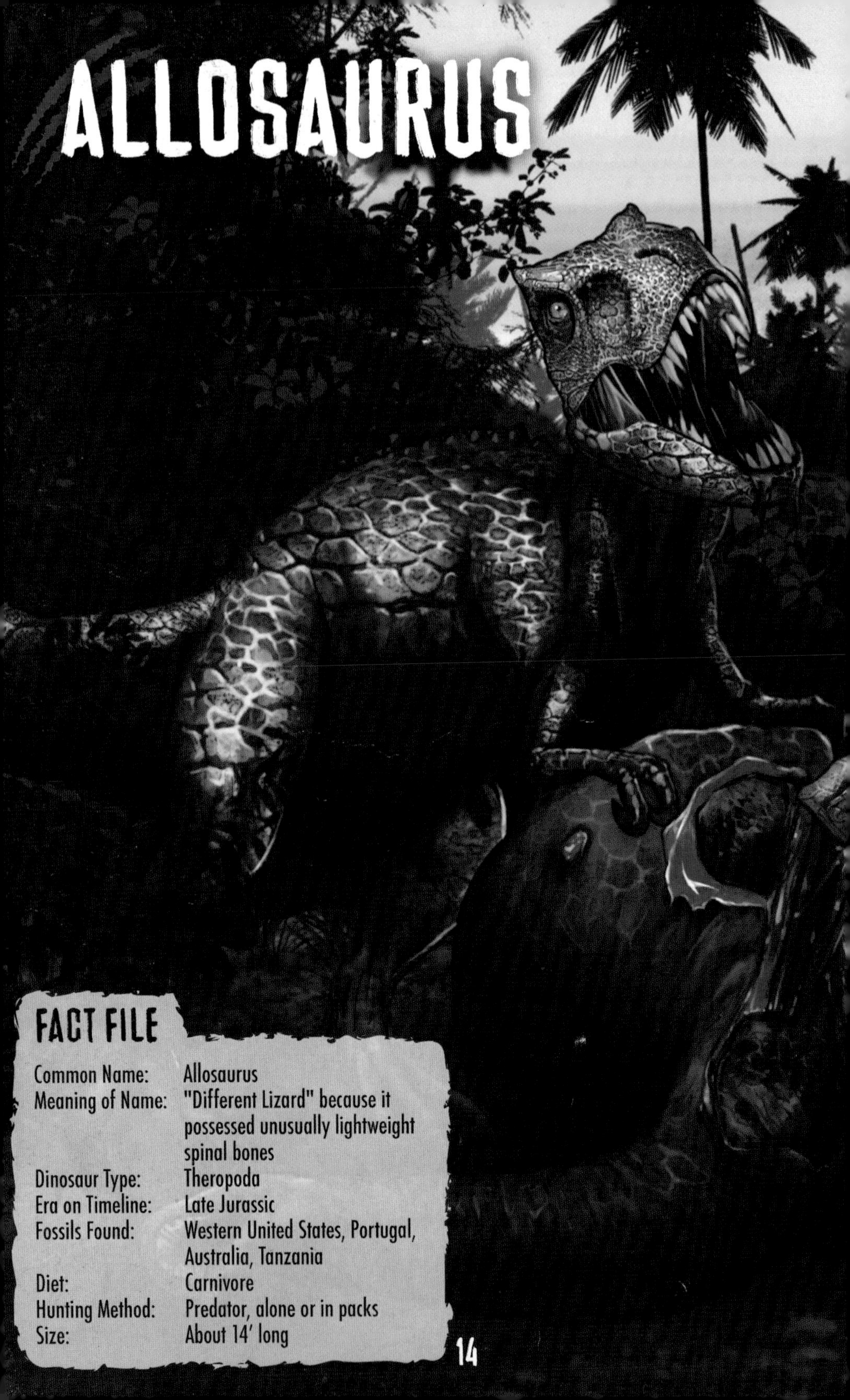

FACT FILE

Common Name:	Allosaurus
Meaning of Name:	"Different Lizard" because it possessed unusually lightweight spinal bones
Dinosaur Type:	Theropoda
Era on Timeline:	Late Jurassic
Fossils Found:	Western United States, Portugal, Australia, Tanzania
Diet:	Carnivore
Hunting Method:	Predator, alone or in packs
Size:	About 14′ long

On the upper jaw it had razor sharp teeth, serrated and curved toward the inside of its mouth.

On the lower jaw, the teeth had a more upright position.

This is so it could hack into flesh with its upper teeth, while its lower teeth could then rip flesh from bone.

THE STORY OF THE MIGHTY **ALLOSAURUS** TOOK PLACE 145 MILLION YEARS AGO.

ONE MIGHT FIND IT HARD TO **IMAGINE** THAT A CREATURE **45 FEET LONG** AND WEIGHING IN AT AROUND **THREE AND A HALF TONS** STARTED ITS LIFE IN AN EGG ABOUT THE SIZE OF A **FOOTBALL.**

FOR THE FIRST FEW WEEKS OF THE NEWBORN'S LIFE HIS MOTHER STAYS **CLOSE** TO PROVIDE **FOOD** AND **PROTECTION.**

IT WON'T BE **LONG** BEFORE THE YOUNG ALLOSAURUS WILL HAVE TO LEARN TO SURVIVE ON HIS **OWN** IN THE **HARSH** AND **TREACHEROUS** WORLD OF DINOSAURS.

ONLY A FEW MONTHS OLD, THE INFANT ALLOSAURUS MUST LEARN HOW TO SURVIVE ON HIS OWN. TO DO THIS HE MUST MASTER TWO VITAL SKILLS. THE FIRST IS TO FIGHT.

THE SECOND IS TO HUNT.

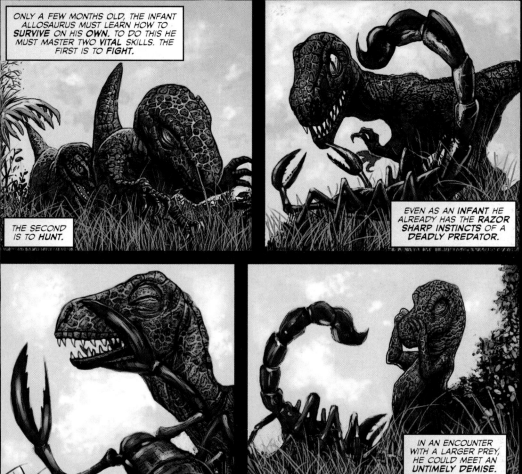

EVEN AS AN INFANT HE ALREADY HAS THE RAZOR SHARP INSTINCTS OF A DEADLY PREDATOR.

INSTINCTS ALONE WON'T BE ENOUGH TO KEEP HIM ALIVE IN A WORLD OF ENDLESS DANGERS.

IN AN ENCOUNTER WITH A LARGER PREY, HE COULD MEET AN UNTIMELY DEMISE.

HE MUST LEARN TO USE HIS SUPERIOR SIZE AND STRENGTH TO HIS ADVANTAGE.

WITH HIS FIRST KILL, HE TASTES THE FLAVOR OF VICTORY.

AND EARNED HIMSELF A TASTY SNACK.

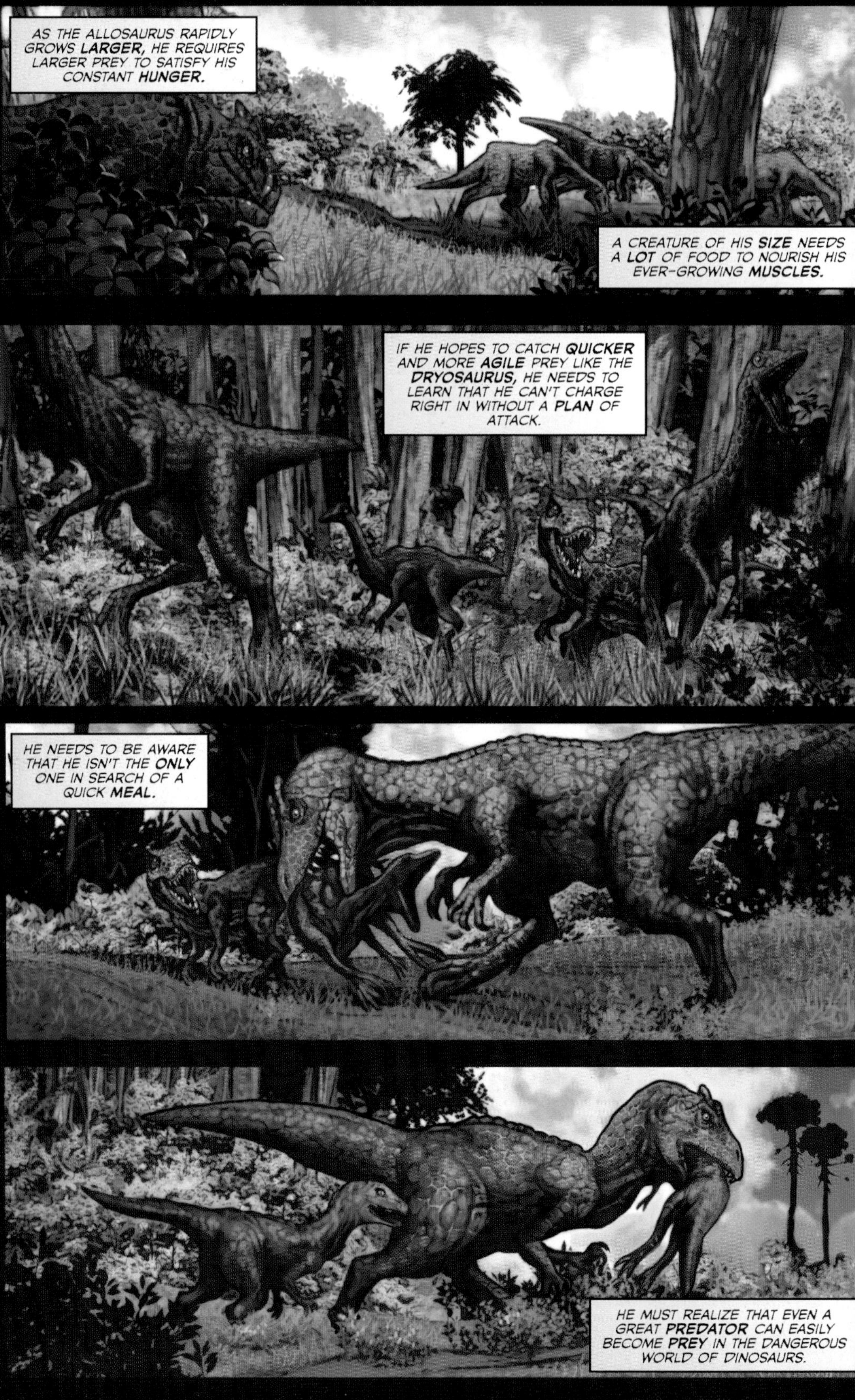
AS THE ALLOSAURUS RAPIDLY GROWS **LARGER,** HE REQUIRES LARGER PREY TO SATISFY HIS CONSTANT **HUNGER.**
A CREATURE OF HIS **SIZE** NEEDS A **LOT** OF FOOD TO NOURISH HIS EVER-GROWING **MUSCLES.**
IF HE HOPES TO CATCH **QUICKER** AND MORE **AGILE** PREY LIKE THE **DRYOSAURUS,** HE NEEDS TO LEARN THAT HE CAN'T CHARGE RIGHT IN WITHOUT A **PLAN** OF ATTACK.
HE NEEDS TO BE AWARE THAT HE ISN'T THE **ONLY** ONE IN SEARCH OF A QUICK **MEAL.**
HE MUST REALIZE THAT EVEN A GREAT **PREDATOR** CAN EASILY BECOME **PREY** IN THE DANGEROUS WORLD OF DINOSAURS.

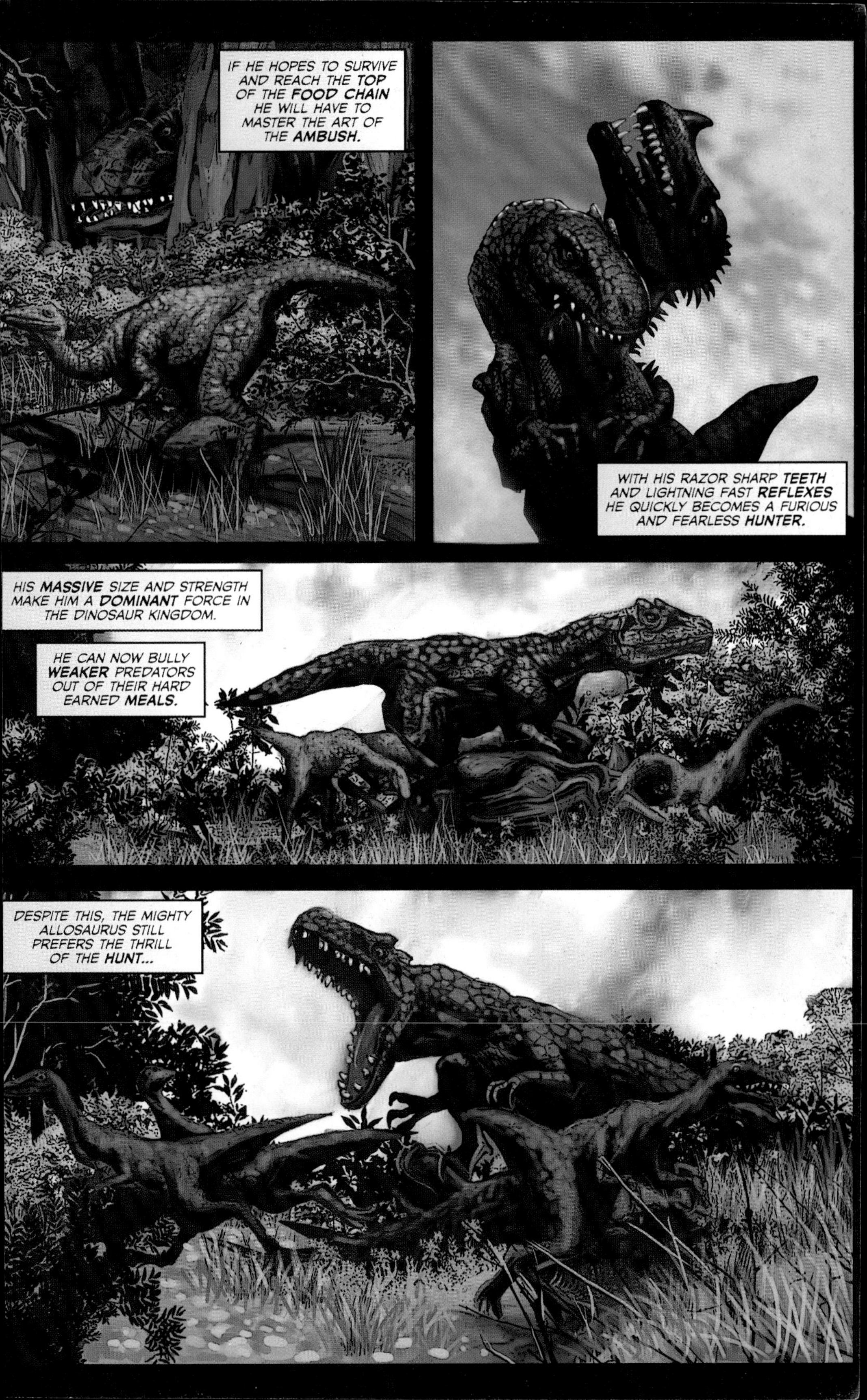
IF HE HOPES TO SURVIVE AND REACH THE TOP OF THE FOOD CHAIN HE WILL HAVE TO MASTER THE ART OF THE AMBUSH.
WITH HIS RAZOR SHARP TEETH AND LIGHTNING FAST REFLEXES HE QUICKLY BECOMES A FURIOUS AND FEARLESS HUNTER.
HIS MASSIVE SIZE AND STRENGTH MAKE HIM A DOMINANT FORCE IN THE DINOSAUR KINGDOM.
HE CAN NOW BULLY WEAKER PREDATORS OUT OF THEIR HARD EARNED MEALS.
DESPITE THIS, THE MIGHTY ALLOSAURUS STILL PREFERS THE THRILL OF THE HUNT...

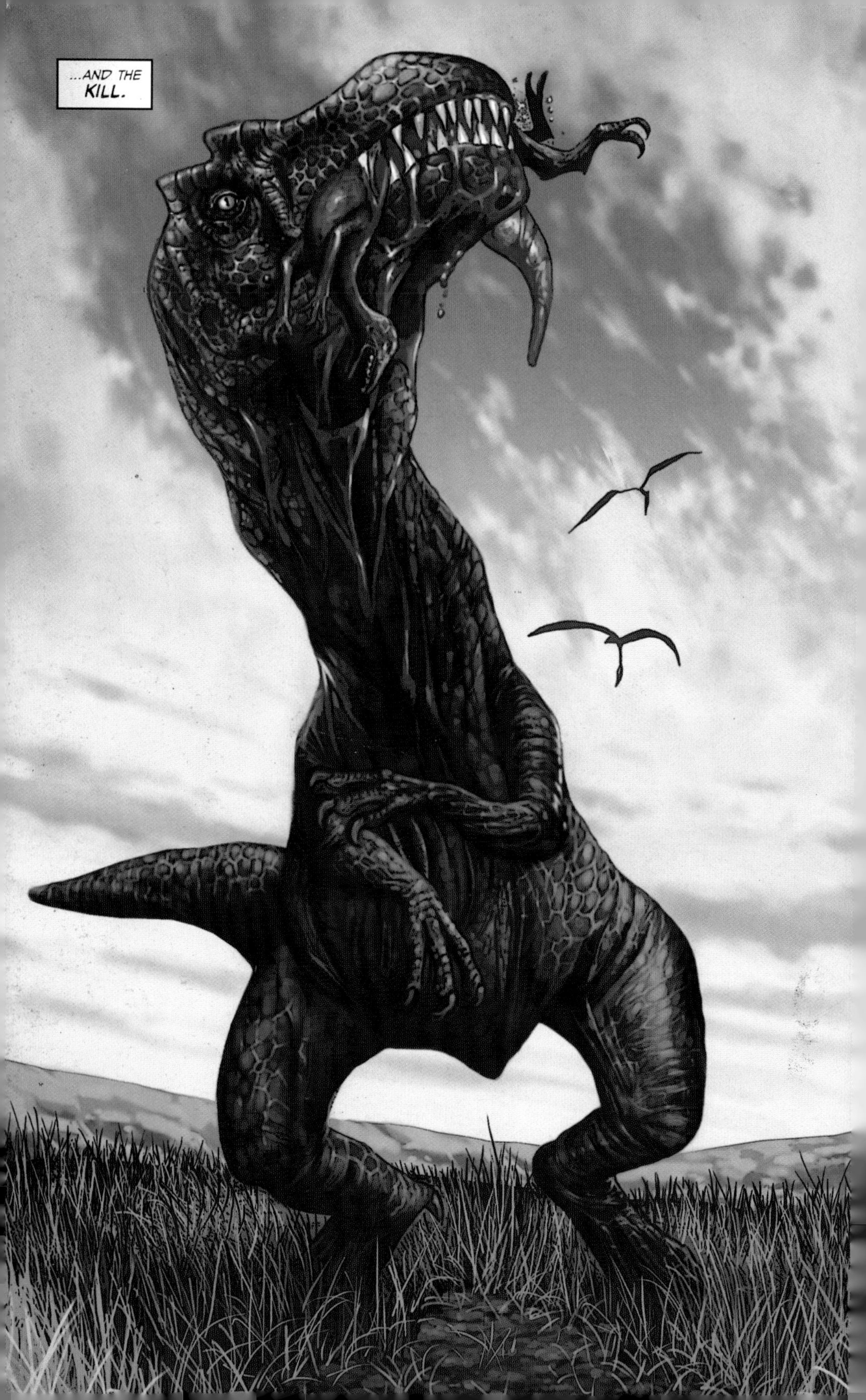
...AND THE KILL.

WHILE HIS MASSIVE SIZE AND POWER MAY BE HIS GREATEST *STRENGTH*, IN THE *DRY SEASON* IT CAN BE HIS *GREATEST WEAKNESS*.

A 30-FOOT ALLOSAURUS WEIGHING 3.5 TONS NEEDS TO DRINK A *LOT* OF WATER TO *SURVIVE*.

WHEN THERE ISN'T MUCH WATER TO GO AROUND, WHAT LITTLE THERE IS BECOMES A *PRIZE* WORTH *FIGHTING* FOR...

...WORTH *DYING* FOR.

HIS CHANCES FOR SURVIVAL ARE NOW GRIM.

THE ONCE MIGHTY PREDATOR HAS BEEN REDUCED TO A SCAVENGER.

WITH SEVERAL BROKEN RIBS AND AN INFECTED LEG, THE ALLOSAURUS IS TOO WEAK TO HUNT FOR A MUCH NEEDED MEAL.

THE HUNGER RUMBLING IN HIS STOMACH HAS BROUGHT HIM TO THE BRINK OF DESPERATION.

THE SMELL OF A FRESHLY DECEASED CERATOSAURUS IS MORE THAN HE CAN RESIST.

HIS MASSIVE SIZE AND WEIGHT ARE HIS FINAL UNDOING.

HE COULD HAVE NEVER KNOWN THAT THE PRICE OF A FREE MEAL WOULD BE HIS OWN LIFE.

145 MILLION YEARS AFTER HIS DEMISE IN THE SWAMP, THE GREAT ALLOSAURUS' **FOSSILIZED REMAINS** WERE **FOUND** BY PALEONTOLOGISTS AND CAREFULLY **REMOVED** FROM THE EARTH.

HE NOW STANDS TALL IN A **MUSEUM** AS A **TRIBUTE** TO THE GREAT **DINOSAURS** THAT ONCE **RULED** THE EARTH.

HE SERVES AS A REMINDER THAT TO SURVIVE IN THE LAND OF DINOSAURS, EVEN THE **GREATEST** PREDATORS LIKE ALLOSAURUS HAD NO CHOICE BUT TO LIVE **HARD** AND **FAST**.

ANKYLOSAURUS

Ankylosaurus was the largest and best known of the armored dinosaurs known as ankylosaurids. All of them had heavily armored bodies and large, clubbed tails.

The only way to attack an Ankylosaurus was to flip the low-slung, armored dinosaur onto its back to get at its unarmored belly — not an easy feat!

Its armored tail club was made up of fused armor plates and was powerful enough to break bones.

FACT FILE

Common Name:	Ankylosaurus
Meaning of Name:	"Fused Lizard"
Dinosaur Type:	Armored
Era on Timeline:	Late Cretaceous
Fossils Found:	Western United States and Alberta, Canada
Diet:	Herbivore
Hunting Method:	Grazer
Size:	25' to 35' long

EARTH, 68 MILLION YEARS AGO ... **ANKLOSAURUS**, A PLANT EATING DINOSAUR OF THE LATE **CRETACEOUS** PERIOD WAS GRAZING AT THE EDGE OF A PREHISTORIC FOREST, TRYING TO SATISFY ITS LARGE **APPETITE**.

SUDDENLY, THE FOREST GREW **SILENT**...

AND A LARGE, MENACING **SHADOW** FELL ACROSS THE HEAVILY-ARMORED DINER.

GIGANOTOSAURUS, ONE OF THE **LARGEST** PREDATORS IN THE WORLD! IT HAD ZEROED IN ON THE SLOW-MOVING ANKYLOSAURUS.

MOST DINOSAURS **RAN** WHEN THEY SPOTTED GIGANOTOSAURUS. BUT **NOT** THE ANKYLOSAURUS. THEY **STOOD** THEIR **GROUND** WHEN CHALLENGED.

THE HUNGRY GIGANOTOSAURUS WAS NOT **IMPRESSED.** THIS SHORT, BEAKED DINOSAUR WAS ABOUT TO BECOME ITS **LUNCH!**

THE GIGANOTOSAURUS **LUNGED,** ITS MASSIVE JAWS WIDE **OPEN,** SEEKING TO SUBDUE ITS **PREY!**

KTHUNK

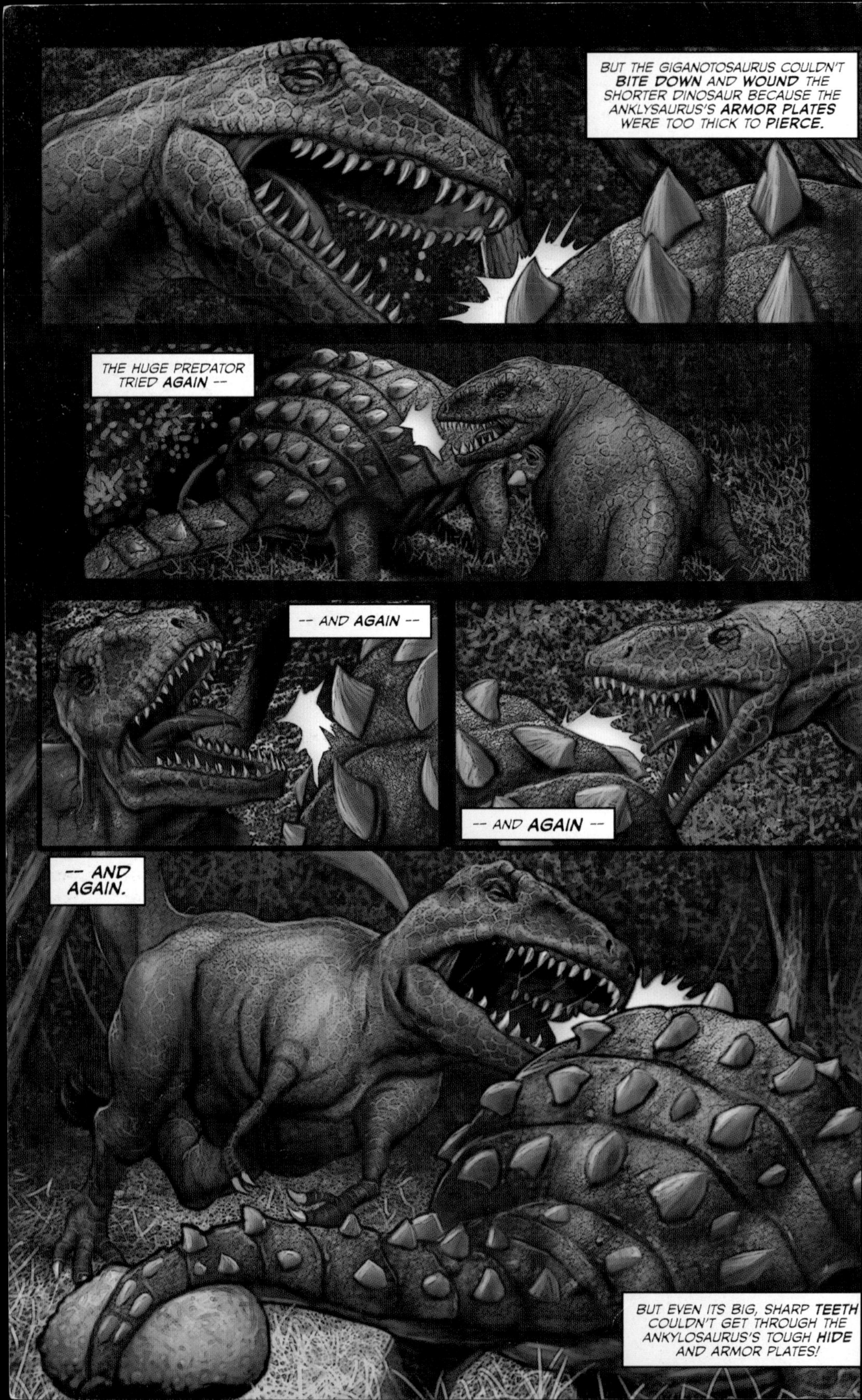
BUT THE GIGANOTOSAURUS COULDN'T BITE DOWN AND WOUND THE SHORTER DINOSAUR BECAUSE THE ANKLYSAURUS'S ARMOR PLATES WERE TOO THICK TO PIERCE.
THE HUGE PREDATOR TRIED AGAIN --
-- AND AGAIN --
-- AND AGAIN --
-- AND AGAIN.
BUT EVEN ITS BIG, SHARP TEETH COULDN'T GET THROUGH THE ANKYLOSAURUS'S TOUGH HIDE AND ARMOR PLATES!

THE GIGANOTOSAURUS REARED IN **PAIN**, SURPRISED BY THE UNEXPECTED ATTACK.

BUT THE PAIN ONLY MADE THE MASSIVE CARNIVORE **ANGRY** -- AND **HUNGRY!**

IT OPENED ITS MASSIVE JAWS AND TRIED TO **BITE** THE FEISTY ANKLOSAURUS AGAIN.

GETTING **NOTHING** FOR ITS TROUBLE BUT A MOUTHFUL OF **ARMOR** AND **SPIKES**.

KRUNK

THAT WAS **ENOUGH** FOR THE GIGANOTOSAURUS. IT KNEW WHEN IT WAS **BEAT**.

IT STORMED OFF IN SEARCH OF **EASIER** PREY.

WHICH WAS **FINE** WITH ANKYLOSAURUS, WHO MERELY WANTED TO FINISH ITS **LUNCH**!

GIGANOTOSAURUS LEARNED WHAT
MANY OF THE TOP PREDATORS OF THE
CRETACEOUS PERIOD LEARNED WHEN
HUNTING... YOU DON'T **CROSS** AN
ANKLOSAURUS WHEN IT'S ENJOYING
ITS MIDDAY **MEAL.**

APATOSAURUS

Apatosaurus didn't **need** to chew its food and could just **eat** and **eat**, **grinding up** their food in a lower portion of their stomach called the **gizzard**.

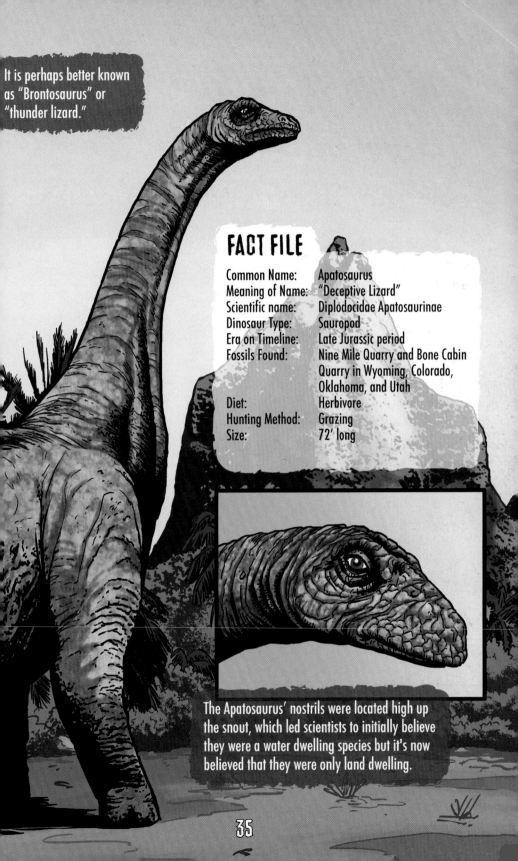

It is perhaps better known as "Brontosaurus" or "thunder lizard."

FACT FILE

Common Name:	Apatosaurus
Meaning of Name:	"Deceptive Lizard"
Scientific name:	Diplodocidae Apatosaurinae
Dinosaur Type:	Sauropod
Era on Timeline:	Late Jurassic period
Fossils Found:	Nine Mile Quarry and Bone Cabin Quarry in Wyoming, Colorado, Oklahoma, and Utah
Diet:	Herbivore
Hunting Method:	Grazing
Size:	72' long

The Apatosaurus' nostrils were located high up the snout, which led scientists to initially believe they were a water dwelling species but it's now believed that they were only land dwelling.

FROM 1877 TO 1892, PALEONTOLOGISTS **OTHNIEL CHARLES MARSH** OF THE PEABODY MUSEUM OF NATURAL HISTORY AT YALE UNIVERSITY --

-- AND **EDWARD DRINKER COPE** OF THE ACADEMY OF NATURAL SCIENCES IN PHILADELPHIA --

-- WERE AT THE CENTER OF ONE OF THE MOST DRAMATIC AND COMPETITIVE PERIODS IN FOSSIL DISCOVERY.

WHILE COPE AND MARSH GOT ALONG AT FIRST, OVER TIME THE DIFFERENCES IN THEIR BACKGROUNDS AND IDEOLOGIES PUSHED THEM APART.

THESE UNEASY COLLEAGUES BECAME HEATED RIVALS NOT LONG AFTER AN EXPEDITION TO A FOSSIL-RICH SITE IN NEW JERSEY.

THOUGH THE SITE WAS ONE FREQUENTED BY COPE, MARSH BRIBED THE PIT OPERATORS TO SEND ALL FUTURE FINDS TO HIM INSTEAD OF COPE.

FROM THEN ON, THE PAIR TOOK EVERY OPPORTUNITY TO EITHER EMBARRASS OR SABOTAGE EACH OTHER.

USING SUCH TACTICS AS ATTACKS IN PAPERS AND PUBLICATIONS, THEFT, AND EVEN DESTRUCTION OF BONES --

-- THESE TWO MEN WERE DETERMINED TO DO WHATEVER IT TOOK TO BE NAMED THE LEADING AUTHORITY IN THE NEW FIELD OF DINOSAUR PALEONTOLOGY.

HOWEVER, EVEN THOUGH THE "BONE WARS" LEFT BOTH MARSH AND COPE PENNILESS AND SOCIAL OUTCASTS --

-- THEIR CONTRIBUTIONS CANNOT BE OVERLOOKED, AS BETWEEN THEM THEY DISCOVERED OVER 142 NEW DINOSAUR SPECIES.

ONE SUCH SPECIES WAS A SAUROPOD THAT MARSH NAMED **BRONTOSAURUS**.

HOWEVER, WHILE THAT NAME REMAINS POPULAR AND WELL-KNOWN, IN HIS RUSH TO BEAT COPE ONCE AGAIN, MARSH MADE A MISTAKE.

INSTEAD OF DISCOVERING A **BRAND-NEW** SPECIES, MARSH HAD FOUND EVIDENCE OF THE ADULT VERSION OF A DINOSAUR HE HAD CATALOGED TWO YEARS EARLIER --

-- THE **APATOSAURUS**.

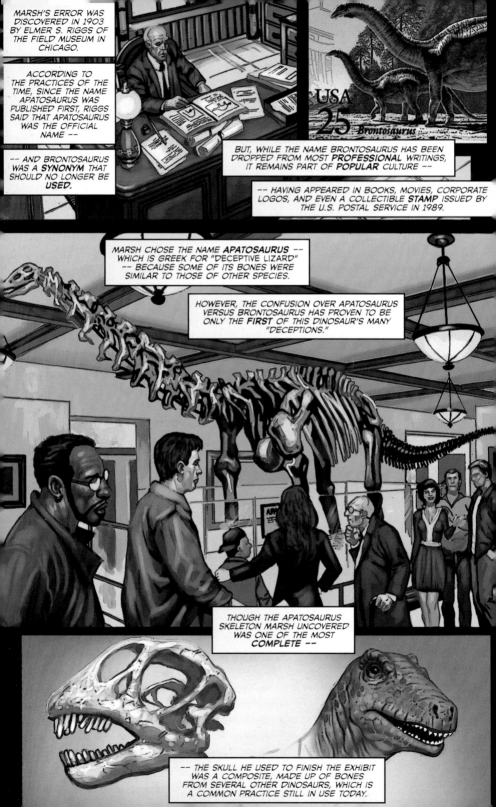

MARSH'S ERROR WAS DISCOVERED IN 1903 BY ELMER S. RIGGS OF THE FIELD MUSEUM IN CHICAGO.

ACCORDING TO THE PRACTICES OF THE TIME, SINCE THE NAME APATOSAURUS WAS PUBLISHED FIRST, RIGGS SAID THAT APATOSAURUS WAS THE OFFICIAL NAME --

-- AND BRONTOSAURUS WAS A SYNONYM THAT SHOULD NO LONGER BE USED.

USA 25 Brontosaurus

BUT, WHILE THE NAME BRONTOSAURUS HAS BEEN DROPPED FROM MOST PROFESSIONAL WRITINGS, IT REMAINS PART OF POPULAR CULTURE --

-- HAVING APPEARED IN BOOKS, MOVIES, CORPORATE LOGOS, AND EVEN A COLLECTIBLE STAMP ISSUED BY THE U.S. POSTAL SERVICE IN 1989.

MARSH CHOSE THE NAME APATOSAURUS -- WHICH IS GREEK FOR "DECEPTIVE LIZARD" -- BECAUSE SOME OF ITS BONES WERE SIMILAR TO THOSE OF OTHER SPECIES.

HOWEVER, THE CONFUSION OVER APATOSAURUS VERSUS BRONTOSAURUS HAS PROVEN TO BE ONLY THE FIRST OF THIS DINOSAUR'S MANY "DECEPTIONS."

THOUGH THE APATOSAURUS SKELETON MARSH UNCOVERED WAS ONE OF THE MOST COMPLETE --

-- THE SKULL HE USED TO FINISH THE EXHIBIT WAS A COMPOSITE, MADE UP OF BONES FROM SEVERAL OTHER DINOSAURS, WHICH IS A COMMON PRACTICE STILL IN USE TODAY.

LIKE OTHER EARLY PALEONTOLOGISTS, MARSH ASSUMED THAT SAUROPODS WERE NOT LAND CREATURES BECAUSE THEY APPEARED TOO WEAK TO SUPPORT THEIR OWN WEIGHT.

INSTEAD, IT WAS BELIEVED APATOSAURUS AND OTHER SAUROPODS LIVED IN SHALLOW LAKES AND SWAMPS SO THEY COULD USE THE **WATER** TO FLOAT THEIR MASSIVE **BULK.**

HOWEVER, THIS IS NO LONGER A **SUPPORTED** THEORY, AS NO SAUROPOD FOSSILS HAVE BEEN UNEARTHED IN ANCIENT BODIES OF WATER.

ALSO, THE FOOT BONES THAT HAVE BEEN FOUND SHOW THAT THEY WERE NOT **SUITED** FOR WALKING THROUGH THE MUDDY TERRAIN OF **MARSHLAND.**

THE **CURRENT** BELIEF IS THAT APATOSAURUS MADE ITS HOME IN **DRY** FLOODPLAINS.

IN FACT, SOME SCIENTISTS THINK THAT WHEN THEIR TERRITORY GOT **WET,** APATOSAURUS WOULD MOVE SOMEWHERE **ELSE!**

CONSIDERING ITS MASSIVE SIZE, IT'S EASY TO BELIEVE THE IMAGE OF A WEAK, PLODDING DINOSAUR APATOSAURUS HAS HAD SINCE ITS DISCOVERY.

HOWEVER, PALEONTOLOGISTS LIKE ROBERT BAKKER -- CURRENT CURATOR OF PALEONTOLOGY AT THE HOUSTON MUSEUM OF NATURAL SCIENCE AND ONE WHO PREFERS THE MORE POPULAR "BRONTOSAURUS" -- THINK DIFFERENTLY.

BAKKER AND OTHERS BELIEVE THAT APATOSAURUS WAS ACTUALLY MUCH **MORE ACTIVE** THAN ORIGINALLY THOUGHT --

-- AND THAT IT WAS ABLE TO STAND ON ITS HIND LEGS, USING ITS TAIL AS A BALANCING "THIRD LEG" IN ORDER TO GRAZE HIGH BRANCHES.

THIS COULD EVEN MEAN THAT MALES WOULD REA UP IN A **SIMILAR** FASHIO TO **INTIMIDATE** RIVALS DURING **MATING**.

ALSO CONTRIBUTING TO THE IDEA OF APATOSAURUS AS A SLOW, WEAK DINOSAUR IS THE RELATIVE SIZE OF ITS HEAD TO ITS BODY --

-- AND HOW IT SEEMED TOO **SMALL** TO EAT ENOUGH TO FUEL ITS **HUGE** BODY.

BUT, WHILE ITS HEAD COULD EAT ENOUGH TO FUEL ITSELF, IT WASN'T BIG ENOUGH TO HOLD A VERY LARGE **BRAIN.**

THOUGH SOME HAVE THEORIZED THAT APATOSAURUS HAD A **SECOND** BRAIN AT THE BASE OF ITS SPINAL CORD, IT AND OTHER SAUROPODS ARE CONSIDERED SOME OF THE **LEAST INTELLIGENT** DINOSAURS.

ONE MIGHT THINK THAT ITS LACK OF INTELLIGENCE WOULD MAKE APATOSAURUS AN **EASY** MEAL FOR PREDATORS, LIKE THE **ALLOSAURUS...**

...HOWEVER APATOSAURUS WAS **FAR** FROM DEFENSELESS.

CAREFUL RECONSTRUCTION OF THE APATORSAURUS'S TAIL HAS SHOWN THAT IT COULD BE SWUNG IN **WHIP-LIKE** FASHION TO FIGHT OFF POTENTIAL THREATS.

THWAK

ALSO, MOST PREDATORY DINOSAURS PREFERRED TO ATTACK THE **NECK** OR **HEAD** OF ITS PREY --

-- AND SINCE BOTH WERE VERY HIGH OFF THE GROUND ON APATOSAURUS, NOT TO MENTION AN ATTACKER WOULD HAVE TO GET PAST THE TAIL FIRST, THIS WAS **VERY** DIFFICULT TO DO.

THERE ARE STILL **SEVERAL** MYSTERIES ABOUT THE APATOSAURUS THAT REMAIN UNSOLVED.

FOR EXAMPLE, WHETHER APATOSAURUS WAS A **SOLITARY** DINOSAUR...

...OR LIVED IN **HERDS.**

REGARDLESS, APATOSAURUS -- OR **BRONTOSAURUS,** IF YOU PREFER -- REMAINS ONE OF THE MOST **RECOGNIZED** AND **POPULAR** DINOSAURS THAT HAS EVER BEEN DISCOVERED.

PTERANODON

Pteranodons are the best known member of the Pterosaur family, and the most common. Their most distinctive characteristic is their bony head crest.

They had hollow bones, which is why they were so light and so tall.

FACT FILE

Common Name:	Pteranodon
Meaning of Name:	"Winged finger"
Dinosaur Type:	Pteranodons are not actually dinosaurs—they are winged reptiles
Era on Timeline:	Late Cretaceous
Fossils Found:	Midwestern United States (Kansas) and England
Diet:	Carnivore, scavenger
Hunting Method:	Scooped fish and mollusks out of the water, dug crabs and mollusks up from the shore
Size:	6' tall with a 25' to 35' wingspan

For years scientists thought Pteranodons, and pterosaurs in general, could only glide, but recent discoveries have shown that they could fly under their own power.

MOST PTERODACTYLS WERE **PACK** ANIMALS. THEY OFTEN TRAVELED IN LARGE **FLOCKS**, JUST LIKE MODERN-DAY **BIRDS**.

THE MOST COMMON TYPE WAS **PTERANODON LONGICEPS.** IT WAS ALSO ONE OF THE **LARGEST** PTERODACTYLS.

THE PTERANODONS LIVED IN ARGE COMMUNAL NESTS, OR **ROOKERIES,** THEY CREATED ON ROCKS RISING FROM THE WATER.

LIVING AWAY FROM **LAND** KEPT THEM **SAFE** FROM OTHER PREDATORY DINOSAURS.

AND LIVING SO **HIGH** UP KEPT THEM SAFE FROM CREATURES **IN** THE WATER ITSELF.

THE ONLY **PROBLEM** WAS, THERE WASN'T ANYTHING TO **EAT** ON THE ROOKERY!

SO WHEN THEY WERE **HUNGRY**, THE PTERANODONS HEADED TOWARD THE WATER'S **EDGE**, AND THE LAND JUST BEYOND.

THEY TRIED TO **SCOOP UP** FISH ON THE WAY, BUT THAT DIDN'T ALWAYS **WORK**.

PREHISTORIC FISH WERE OFTE BIGGER AND HEAVIER THAN THE PTERANODONS -- AND **MANY** O THEM HAD **ARMOR PLATES** AN **SHARP TEETH!**

THE PTERANODONS USUALLY HAD TO **LAND** IN ORDER TO **EAT.**

FORTUNATELY, THE PTERANODONS COULD **FOLD** THEIR **WINGS** AND UPPER LEGS **UNDER** THEIR BODY SO THEY COULD **WALK** ON LAND.

EARLIER PTERADACTYLS COULDN'T DO THAT -- THEY HAD **BROADER** WING AND LARGE REAR WING MEMBRANES THAT PINNED THEIR HIND LEGS TO THE **GROUND.** THIS FORCED THEM TO DRAG THEIR LEGS BEHIND THEM MAKING WALKING SLOW AND **DIFFICULT.**

THE PTERANODONS USED THEIR LONG, POINTED **BEAKS** TO SEARCH FOR FOOD. THEY DIDN'T HAVE **TEETH**: "PTERANODON" ACTUALLY MEANS "WINGED AND TOOTHLESS."

AND SOMETIMES THEY MANAGED TO DIG UP **CLAMS** AND OTHER **MOLLUSKS**. THESE MOLLUSKS OFTEN **BURIED** THEMSELVES A FEW **FEET** BELOW THE SURFACE, BUT THE PTERANODONS USED THEIR **BEAKS** TO **UNEARTH** THE TASTY CREATURES.

SOMETIMES THEY CAUGHT **FISH**, AIMING FOR SMALLER SPECIES THAT WOULDN'T PUT UP TOO MUCH OF A **FIGHT**.

SOMETIMES THEY CAUGHT **CRABS**. THESE CRABS LOOKED A LOT LIKE THE **HERMIT CRABS** PEOPLE KEEP AS PETS **TODAY**.

IT COULD TAKE A **WHILE**, AND REQUIRED **PATIENCE** AND **SHARP EYES**. BUT THE PTERANODONS USUALLY FOUND **SOMETHING** TO EAT.

SOMETIMES, THOUGH, THE PTERANODONS FOUND *THEMSELVES* BEING EYED FOR LUNCH *INSTEAD!*

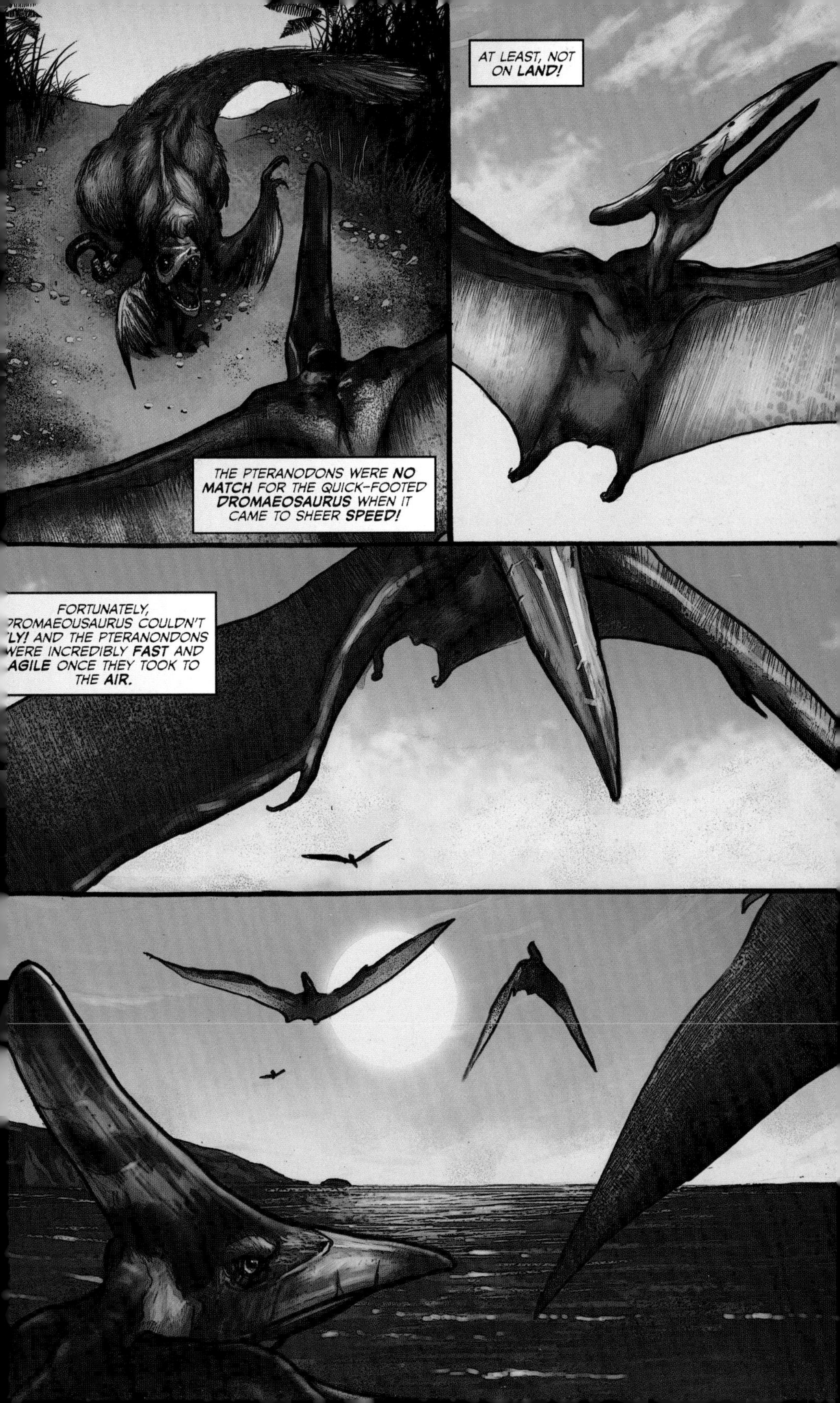

THE PTERANODONS WERE NO MATCH FOR THE QUICK-FOOTED DROMAEOSAURUS WHEN IT CAME TO SHEER SPEED!
AT LEAST, NOT ON LAND!
FORTUNATELY, ROMAEOUSAURUS COULDN'T LY! AND THE PTERANONDONS WERE INCREDIBLY FAST AND AGILE ONCE THEY TOOK TO THE AIR.

THE FLOCK LEFT THE BEACH TO THE DROMAEOSAURUS AND HEADED **BACK** TO THE ROOKERY.

THE PTERANODONS DIDN'T MIND -- THEY'D EATEN THEIR **FILL**, AND WERE READY TO **REST** AND **DIGEST**.

TOO BAD THE **DROMAEOSAURUS** COULDN'T SAY THE **SAME!**

FACT FILE

The Pteranodon has been discovered in Kansas and England, with the first such fossils found by Othneil C. Marsh in 1876. However, the first Pteranodon skull was found in Kansas the same year by S. W. Williston, who was working for Marsh!

SARCOSUCHUS

The wide bulla or bulb at the end of Sarcosuchus snout gave it enough leverage to bring down medium-sized dinosaurs.

With its upward-bulging eyes, Sarcosuchus was able to submerge itself in shallow water and wait for prey to approach from land, then lunge up to attack. Modern-day crocodiles use the same technique.

ACT FILE

ommon Name:	SuperCroc
eaning of Name:	"Flesh crocodile emperor"
cientific Name:	Sarcosuchus Imperator
inosaur Type:	Crocodilian
ra on Timeline:	Early to Middle Cretaceous
ossils Found:	Sahara Desert
iet:	Carnivore
unting Method:	Predator, attacking land-based creatures from shallow water; swimming after and attacking marine creatures, including fish, underwater.
ze:	37' to 40' long

Sarcosuchus had a bite force of 18,000 lbf — that's eighteen thousand pounds of force!

DURING THE **CRETACEOUS** PERIOD, THE **SAHARA** DESERT WAS A SERIES OF WIDE, WET **PLAINS** BROKEN UP BY BROAD, DEEP, SLOW **RIVERS.**

ALL SORTS OF **ANIMALS** -- MAMMALS **AND** DINOSAURS -- LIVED ALONG THE **RIVERBANKS.**

AND MORE LIVED **BENEATH** THE WATER'S **SURFACE.**

ONE OF THE **FIERCEST** RESIDENTS DURING THIS PERIOD WAS THE **SARCOSUCHUS IMPERATOR,** NICKNAMED **SUPERCROC!**

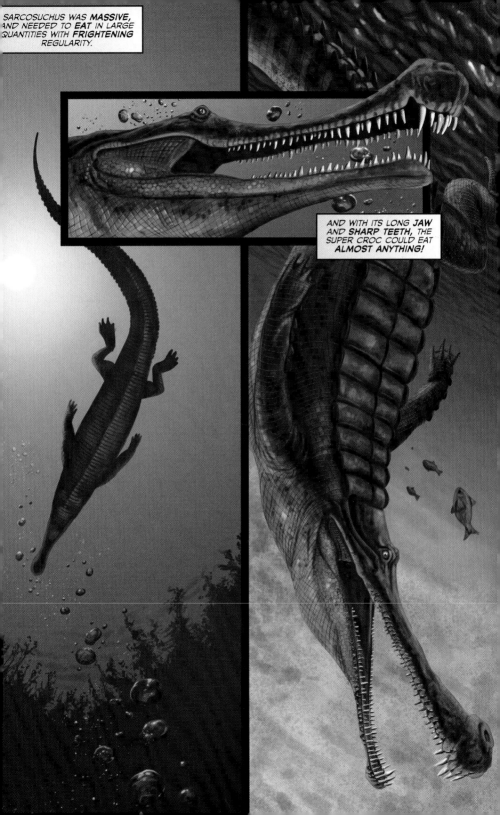

SARCOSUCHUS WAS **MASSIVE,** AND NEEDED TO **EAT** IN LARGE QUANTITIES WITH **FRIGHTENING** REGULARITY.

AND WITH ITS LONG **JAW** AND **SHARP TEETH,** THE SUPER CROC COULD EAT **ALMOST ANYTHING!**

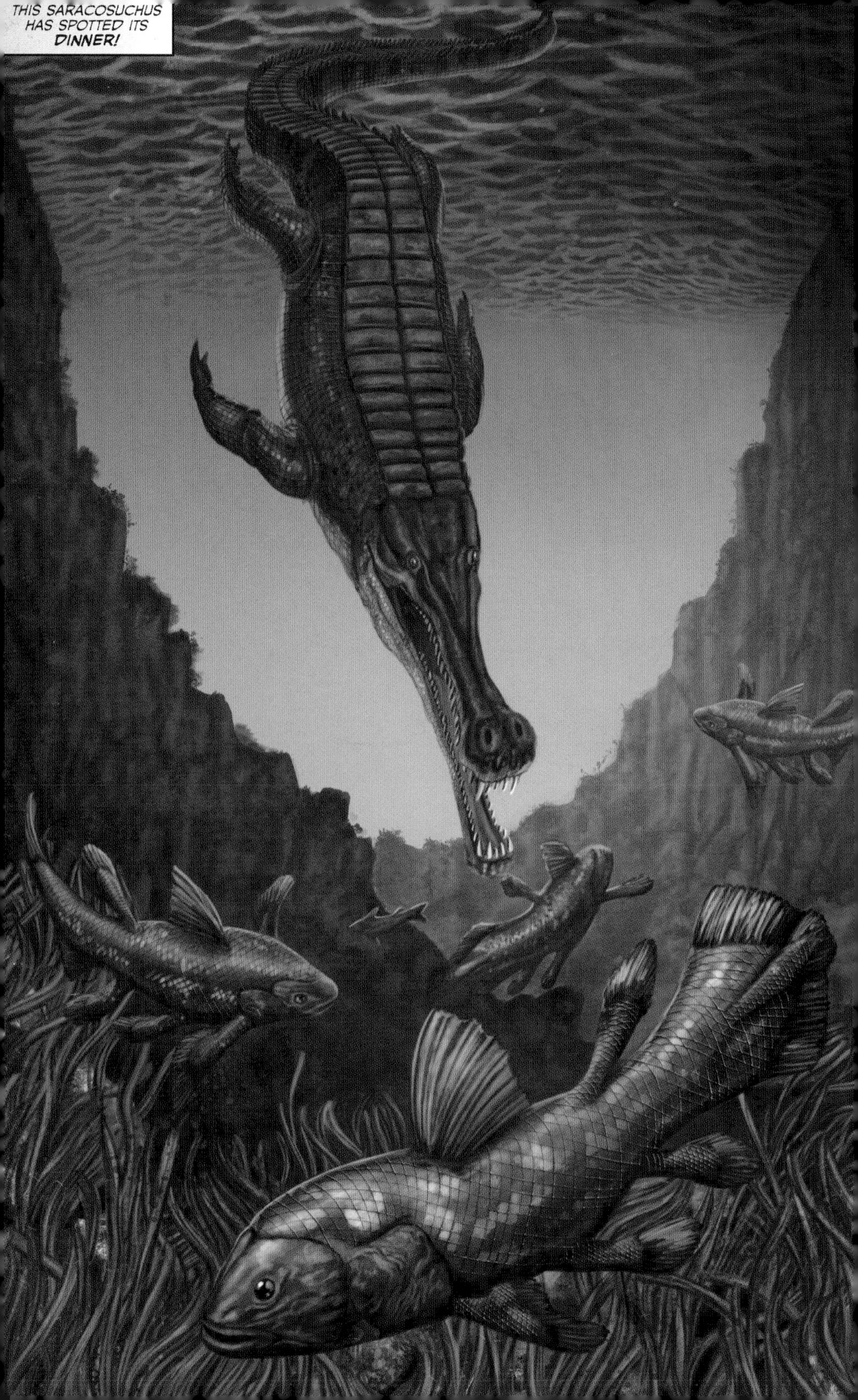
THIS SARACOSUCHUS HAS SPOTTED ITS DINNER!

TAKING OFF **AFTER** THE FISH...

ITS **POWERFUL** TAIL PROPELS IT **RAPIDLY** THROUGH THE WATER.

SENSING THE APPROACH OF THE MASSIVE PREDATOR THE SCHOOL OF MUCH SMALLER PREY FISH **SCATTERS**, **ROBBING** THE SUPER CROC OF AN EASY **MEAL.**

NO MATTER.
SARCOSUCHUS WOULD
JUST HUNT THEM DOWN
ONE AT A TIME.

THE FISH WAS
FAST, BUT **SO** WAS
SARCOSUCHUS.

SARCOSUCHUS
WAS JUST ABOUT TO
FEAST WHEN --

SARCOSUCHUS WAS **FURIOUS** AT HAVING ITS MEAL **SNATCHED** BY THE JAWS OF A RIVAL PREDATOR.

BUT ITS RIVAL WASN'T **CAUGHT** SO **EASILY**.

FORTUNATELY, SUPER CROC WAS NOT FUSSY -- IT WOULD SETTLE FOR THE **LONG-NECKED SUCHOMIMUS** INSTEAD.

THE TWO PREDATORS TRADED **BLOWS**. BOTH WERE ARMED WITH LONG **JAWS** FILLED WITH **SHARP TEETH**.

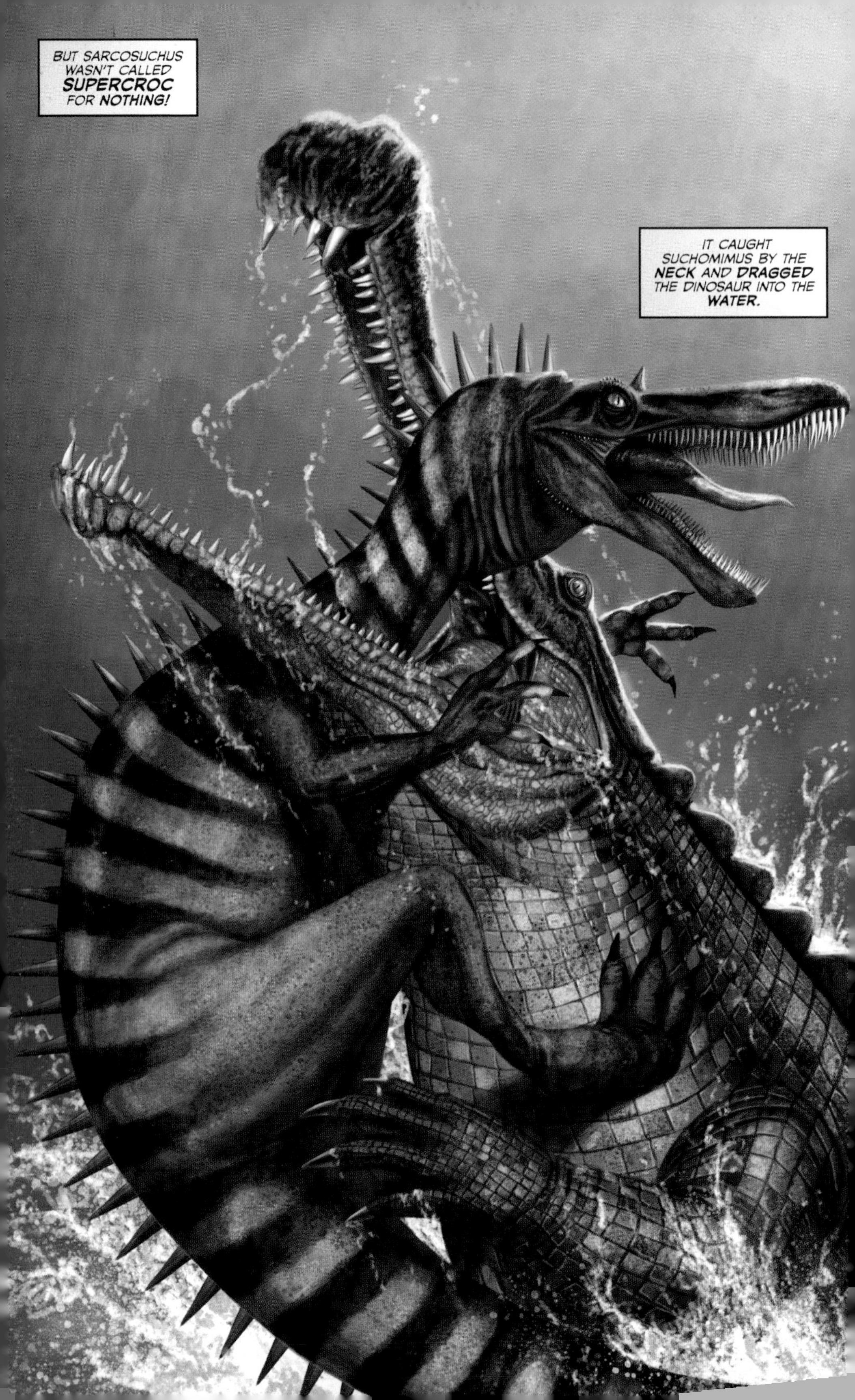
BUT SARCOSUCHUS WASN'T CALLED **SUPERCROC** FOR **NOTHING!**
IT CAUGHT SUCHOMIMUS BY THE **NECK** AND **DRAGGED** THE DINOSAUR INTO THE **WATER.**

SUCHOMIMUS **STRUGGLED.** BUT IT COULDN'T **BREAK FREE!**

UNDERWATER, SARCOSUCHUS WAS **KING.**

SUPER CROC **FINISHED OFF** ITS RIVAL -- AND THEN FINALLY HAD ITS **MEAL.**

IN THE CRETACEOUS WORLD OF SUPER PREDATORS...

IT'S **GOOD** TO BE THE **KING!**

SPINOSAURUS

Unlike other dinosaur predators that had sharp, serrated teeth like the T-Rex, the Spinosaurus' were smooth and round along the length of the tooth.

Spinosaurus had a head larger and longer than any other carnivorous dinosaur. Its jaw, measuring six-feet in length, was very similar to a modern day crocodile.

The sail on the back of the Spinosaurus was fused directly into the creature's vertebra. Paleontologists believe it helped to regulate body temperature of the massive giant.

Blood flowed through vessels in the sail and could be cooled or heated as needed.

FACT FILE

Common Name:	Spinosaurus
Meaning of Name:	"Spiny Lizard"
Dinosaur Type:	Theropoda
Era on Timeline:	Middle Cretaceous
Fossils Found:	Egypt, Morocco, Republic of Niger
Diet:	Carnivore
Hunting Method:	Predator
Size:	40' to 50' long

SPINOSAURUS WAS THE **BIGGEST** CARNIVOROUS DINOSAUR TO **EVER** WALK THE EARTH.

TOWERING AT **60 FEET** AND WEIGHING IN AT **OVER NINE TONS**, A FULL-GROWN ADULT WAS EVEN **LARGER** THAN THE INFAMOUS T-REX.

COUPLE THAT WITH A TRIO OF **12-INCH RAZOR SHARP CLAWS** ON EACH HAND, THERE WAS NO CREATURE ON EARTH THAT WOULDN'T BE KNOCKED STRAIGHT TO THE **GROUND**.

SPINOSAURUS WAS IN **EVERY** WAY THE **ULTIMATE KILLING MACHINE.**

A SWAT FROM ONE OF ITS MASSIVE **SEVEN-FOOT ARMS** WOULD BE ENOUGH TO KNOCK ANY ENEMY **SENSELESS.**

UNLIKE OTHER CARNIVORES, SPINOSAURUS' TEETH **WEREN'T** DESIGNED TO RIP **THROUGH** BONE AND THICK FLESH.

MUCH LIKE A **CROCODILE,** THE SPINOSAURUS **THRASHED** ITS HEAD AROUND TO VIOLENTLY SHAKE THE **LIFE** OUT OF ITS PREY...

KRAKK

CAUSING THE PREY TO BE RIPPED TO **PIECES** BY ITS **OWN** MASS.

THIS WAS SO THE SPINOSAURUS COULD EAT HIS PREY ONE **PIECE** AT A TIME.

THOOM

BUT IN THIS HOSTILE WORLD
EVEN THE **GREATEST** OF ALL
PREDATORS COULD NOT LIVE
A **CARE-FREE** EXISTENCE.

KRAKKTHOOM

DESPITE HIS MASSIVE SIZE SPINOSAURUS WAS EXTREMELY *FAST*.

PROPELLED BY TWO MASSIVE LEGS BUILT FOR FORWARD LOCOMOTION, HE COULD *OUTRUN* ANY CREATURE ON LAND.

WITH FLEXIBLE FEET AND REINFORCED HIPBONES HE HAD THE AGILITY OF A GOLD MEDAL *GYMNAST*.

SPINOSAURUS' SUPERIOR WILL TO *SURVIVE* MADE HIM AN *UNSTOPPABLE* FORCE IN A *VIOLENT* AND *DEADLY* WORLD.

DURING THE **MIDDLE-CRETACEOUS** ERA THE WORLD WAS UNDERGOING **SEVERE** CLIMATE CHANGES.

VOLCANIC ACTIVITY WAS NOT AT ALL UNCOMMON.

MANY PALEONTOLOGISTS BELIEVE THAT AN EXTREME **INCREASE** IN **TEMPERATURE** MAY HAVE CAUSED THE SPINOSAURUS TO BECOME **EXTINCT.**

SUCH **RAPID** CLIMATE CHANGES WOULD HAVE CAUSED LARGER PLANT EATING PREY LIKE THE **PARALITITAN** TO DIE OFF **FIRST.**

FOR A **HIGH-ENERGY** CREATURE LIKE SPINOSAURUS -- THAT NEEDS TO **EAT** CONSTANTLY -- THE **LACK** OF BIG GAME TO **HUNT** AND FEAS ON COULD HAVE MARKED THE BEGINNING OF THE **END.**

THIS GREAT PREDATOR THAT STOOD **UNCHALLENGED** SUDDENLY FACED HIS **DEMISE** IN THE RAPIDLY CHANGING WORLD.

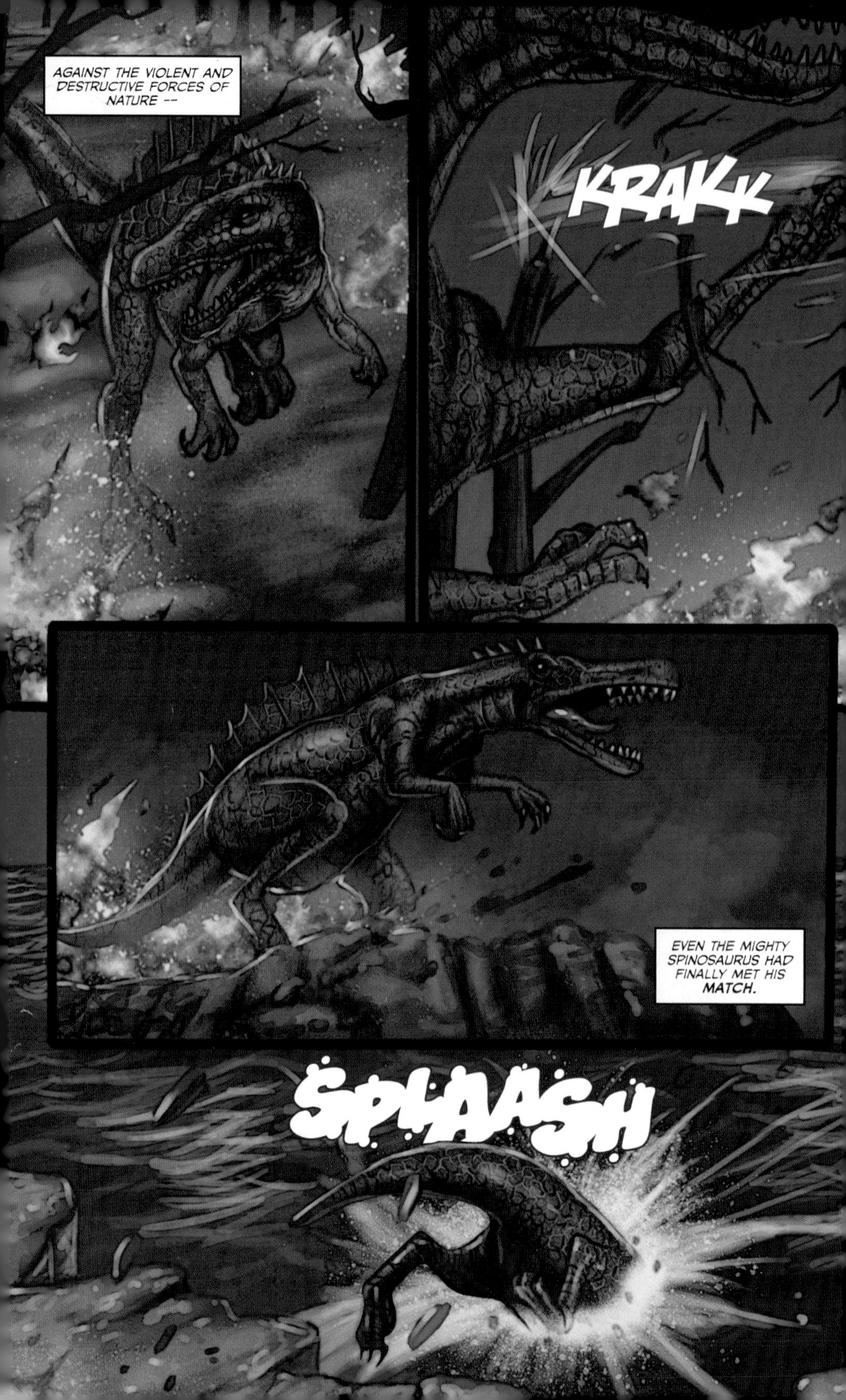
AGAINST THE VIOLENT AND DESTRUCTIVE FORCES OF NATURE --
KRAKK
EVEN THE MIGHTY SPINOSAURUS HAD FINALLY MET HIS MATCH.
SPLAASH

WHILE SPINOSAURUS MAY HAVE BEEN DOOMED TO FALL TO THE COLD HAND OF EXTINCTION, HE WOULD NOT JUST GO QUIETLY INTO THE NIGHT.

WITH ITS SHEER SIZE, SPEED AND STRENGTH, COUPLED WITH AN INDOMITABLE WILL TO SURVIVE, THIS ULTIMATE HUNTER HOLDS A PLACE IN HISTORY AS ONE OF THE GREATEST PREDATORS TO EVER WALK THE EARTH.

STEGOSAURUS

The Stegosaurus grew to an average size of 30 feet long and almost 14 feet tall. Adult males weighed between 5 and 10 tons.

The bony plates running down the back of Stegosaurus likely regulated the giant creature's body heat, but also helped different species identify one another.

Four bony spikes on the end of Stegosaurus' tail made it a formidable opponent.

FACT FILE

Common Name:	Stegosaurus
Meaning of Name:	Narrow-faced Roof Lizard, or Plated Lizard
Scientific Name:	Stegosaurus stenops
Dinosaur Type:	Stegosaur
Era on Timeline:	Late Jurassic Period
Fossils Found:	North America, Europe, and Asia
Diet:	Herbivore
Hunting Method:	Grazer
Size:	26' to 30' long

WYOMING, 145 MILLION YEARS AGO:

SOME 199 TO 140 MILLION YEARS AGO, PLANET EARTH WENT THROUGH THE **JURASSIC PERIOD**, A TIME KNOWN AS THE **AGE OF REPTILES.**

LATE IN THE JURASSIC, THE EARTH WAS SO WARM, THERE WAS NO POLAR ICE CAP, LEAVING THE PLANET COVERED BY TEMPERATE AND SUBTROPICAL FORESTS, GREAT FLOODED PLAINS, AND CORAL REEFS.

INTO THIS ERA THUNDERED THE GREAT DINOSAURS! THE 100-FOOT LONG SUPERSAURUS SHARED THE LANDSCAPE WITH EARLY, SMALL MAMMALS AND BIRDS...

...BUT THE **DOMINANT** DINOSAUR OF THE ERA WAS THE **STEGOSAURUS.** AS MUCH AS 65% OF THE WORLD'S DINOSAUR POPULATION BELONGED TO THIS FAMILY OF GREAT, ARMORED HERBIVORES!

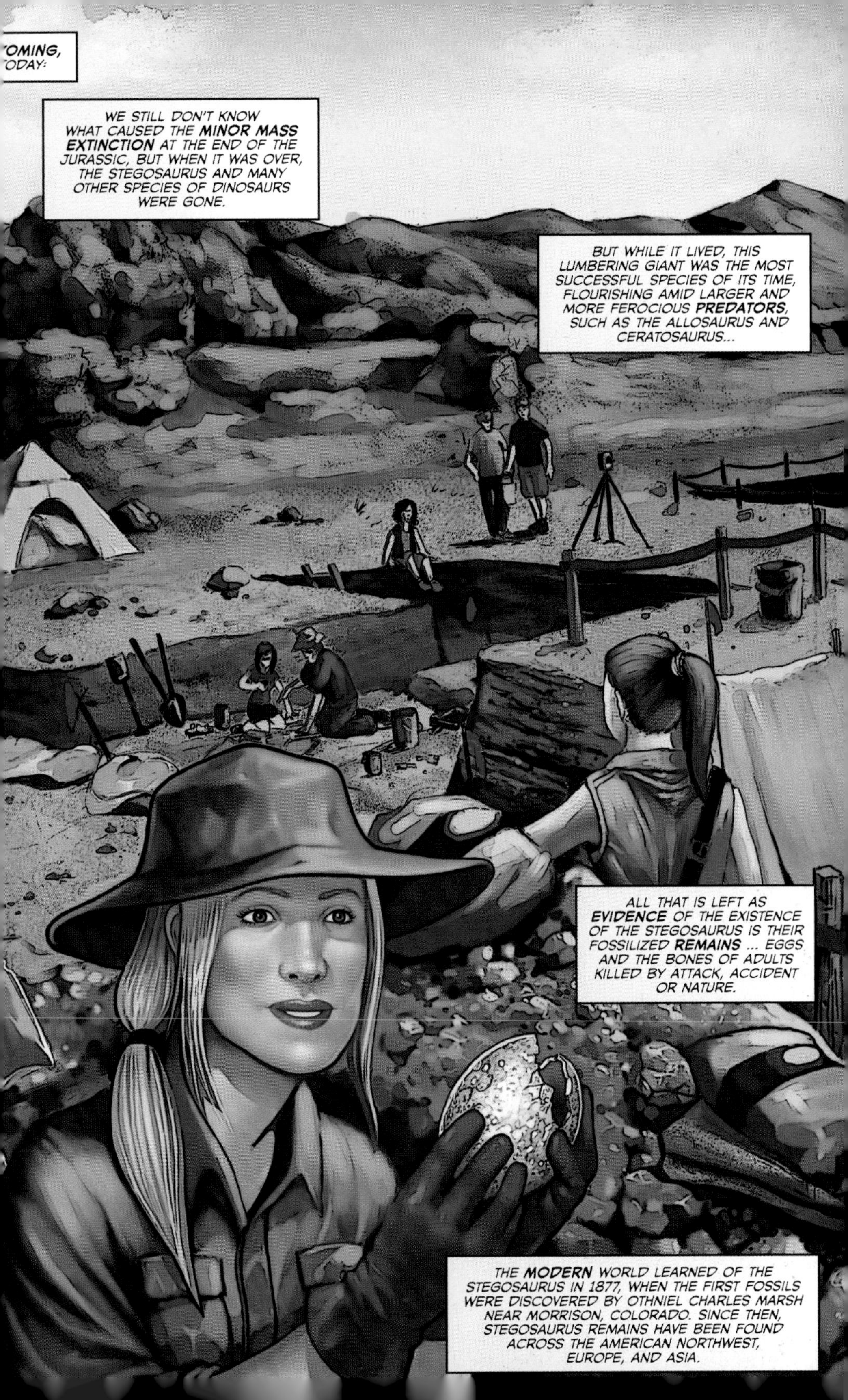
OMING,
ODAY:
WE STILL DON'T KNOW WHAT CAUSED THE **MINOR MASS EXTINCTION** AT THE END OF THE JURASSIC, BUT WHEN IT WAS OVER, THE STEGOSAURUS AND MANY OTHER SPECIES OF DINOSAURS WERE GONE.
BUT WHILE IT LIVED, THIS LUMBERING GIANT WAS THE MOST SUCCESSFUL SPECIES OF ITS TIME, FLOURISHING AMID LARGER AND MORE FEROCIOUS **PREDATORS**, SUCH AS THE ALLOSAURUS AND CERATOSAURUS...
ALL THAT IS LEFT AS **EVIDENCE** OF THE EXISTENCE OF THE STEGOSAURUS IS THEIR FOSSILIZED **REMAINS** ... EGGS AND THE BONES OF ADULTS KILLED BY ATTACK, ACCIDENT OR NATURE.
THE **MODERN** WORLD LEARNED OF THE STEGOSAURUS IN 1877, WHEN THE FIRST FOSSILS WERE DISCOVERED BY OTHNIEL CHARLES MARSH NEAR MORRISON, COLORADO. SINCE THEN, STEGOSAURUS REMAINS HAVE BEEN FOUND ACROSS THE AMERICAN NORTHWEST, EUROPE, AND ASIA.

BUT FOSSILS CAN ONLY TELL US SO MUCH ABOUT A CREATURE THAT LIVED SO LONG AGO.

THE **REST** OF THE STORY WE HAVE HAD TO **SURMISE**, BASED ON THE EVIDENCE DUG FROM THE EARTH...

...SUCH AS HOW THEY WOULD LAY THEIR EGGS IN SHALLOW HOLES SCRATCHED INTO THE GROUND.

STEGOSAURUS EGGS WERE ABOUT THE SIZE OF A SMALL GRAPEFRUIT. FROM THEM WOULD HATCH **SMALL** REPTILES --

-- WHICH WOULD GROW INTO **30-FOOT LONG, 5-TON BEHEMOTHS,** COVERED IN BONY ARMOR PLATING AND PROTECTED BY A SPIKED TAIL IT COULD WIELD LIKE A **CLUB!**

DESPITE ITS SIZE AND **NUMBERS,** STEGOSAURUS STENOPS -- ONE OF MANY FAMILIES OF STEGOSAURIDAE OR "PLATED LIZARDS" -- DID NOT **RULE** THE PREHISTORIC LANDSCAPE

STEGOSAURUS WAS PROBABLY A **HERD** ANIMAL, LIVING IN GROUPS FOR THE SAFETY AND PROTECTION OF ITS **YOUNG** FROM LARGER PREDATORS.

PALEONTOLOGISTS STILL DON'T KNOW WHETHER BABY DINOSAURS HAD TO BE **SELF-SUFFICIENT** RIGHT AFTER HATCHING...

...OR IF, LIKE MODERN-DAY **BIRDS**, ADULTS WATCHED OVER THE NEST AND BROUGHT FOOD TO THE HATCHLINGS.

REGARDLESS, BABY STEGOSAURUS WOULD HAVE HAD TO GROW UP PRETTY QUICKLY TO SURVIVE ITS HARSH ENVIRONMENT.

FORTUNATELY, THERE WAS PLENTY OF FOOD TO FUEL THEIR GROWTH. STEGOSAURUS WAS A **HERBIVORE,** OR PLANT-EATER.

THE TROPICAL LANDSCAPE WAS LUSH WITH VEGETATION, INCLUDING **FERNS,** MOSSES, AND CONIFERS, WHICH ARE CONE-BEARING TREES OR SHRUBS, LIKE A MODERN **PINE TREE.**

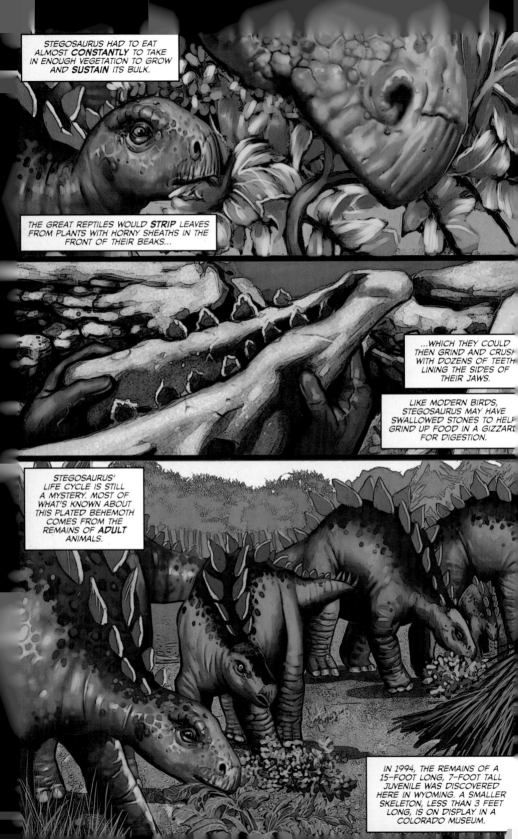

STEGOSAURUS HAD TO EAT ALMOST **CONSTANTLY** TO TAKE IN ENOUGH VEGETATION TO GROW AND **SUSTAIN** ITS BULK.

THE GREAT REPTILES WOULD **STRIP** LEAVES FROM PLANTS WITH HORNY SHEATHS IN THE FRONT OF THEIR BEAKS...

...WHICH THEY COULD THEN GRIND AND CRUSH WITH DOZENS OF TEETH LINING THE SIDES OF THEIR JAWS.

LIKE MODERN BIRDS, STEGOSAURUS MAY HAVE SWALLOWED STONES TO HELP GRIND UP FOOD IN A GIZZARD FOR DIGESTION.

STEGOSAURUS' LIFE CYCLE IS STILL A MYSTERY. MOST OF WHAT'S KNOWN ABOUT THIS PLATED BEHEMOTH COMES FROM THE REMAINS OF **ADULT** ANIMALS.

IN 1994, THE REMAINS OF A 15-FOOT LONG, 7-FOOT TALL JUVENILE WAS DISCOVERED HERE IN WYOMING. A SMALLER SKELETON, LESS THAN 3 FEET LONG, IS ON DISPLAY IN A COLORADO MUSEUM.

THE MOST STARTLING FEATURE OF STEGOSAURUS STENOPS WERE THE **BONY PLATES** THAT RAN DOWN ITS BACK IN 17 ROWS OF TWO.

THEY SEEMED TO HAVE SERVED MANY PURPOSES, INCLUDING REGULATING **BODY TEMPERATURE** BY ABSORBING SOLAR HEAT WHEN STEGOSAURUS NEEDED WARMTH, OR SHEDDING EXCESS HEAT WHEN IT WAS TOO WARM.

THE PLATES MAY HAVE ALSO ALLOWED STEGOSAURUS TO IDENTIFY MEMBERS OF ITS OWN SPECIES, PLAYED A PART IN **COURTSHIP**, AND MADE IT LOOK **BIGGER** TO ENEMIES.

ANOTHER DEFENSIVE FEATURE WAS ITS GREAT, LONG TAIL TOPPED WITH **4 BONY SPIKES** THAT COULD SMASH AN ATTACKER WITH BONE-CRUSHING FORCE.

STEGOSAURUS HAD POWERFUL LEGS TO SUPPORT ITS GREAT WEIGHT. ITS FRONT LEGS WERE SHORTER THAN ITS REAR LEGS, AND IT WAS A QUADRUPED.

SOME BELIEVE IT COULD REAR ON ITS HIND LEGS TO REACH VEGETATION IN HIGHER PLACES, BUT THE COMMON WISDOM IS AGAINST THIS THEORY.

WITH THE REMAINS OF SO FEW JUVENILES EVER FOUND, A YOUNG STEGOSAURUS' CHANCES OF SURVIVAL TO ADULTHOOD SEEMED GOOD.

BUT THE ODDS APPEAR TO CHANGE AS IT REACHED MATURITY!

THERE WAS THE CONSTAN THREAT OF ATTACK BY CARNIVORES, BOTH LARG AND SMALL, DEMANDING DEFENSE BY THE HERD' MALES.

STEGOSAURUS ALSO HAD PROTECTIVE EXTERNAL SCALES CALLED **SCUTES** ON ITS NECK AND HIPS...

...BUT EVEN THESE WERE OFTEN NO MATCH FOR THE JAWS OF THE ERA'S GIANT PREDATORS!

MEASUREMENTS OF STEGOSAURUS SKULLS SHOW THAT THEIR BRAINS WERE TINY, ABOUT THE SIZE OF A WALNUT.

AND YET, STEGOSAURUS WAS A CREATURE PERFECTLY ADAPTED TO ITS ENVIRONMENT...

...GONE NOW, NOT THROUGH ANY FAULT OF ITS OWN, BUT BECAUSE OF AN ENVIRONMENTAL EVENT THAT WIPED OUT UNCOUNTABLE SPECIES.

IF NOT FOR THAT EVENT, THEN STEGOSAURUS AND THE REST OF THE DENIZENS OF THE AGE OF REPTILES MIGHT VERY WELL **STILL** RULE OUR PLANET.

TYRANNOSAURUS REX

Tyrannosaurus Rex's arms were only about 3 feet long but were very strong and may have helped the T-Rex hold onto struggling prey.

FACT FILE

Common Name:	Tyrannosaurus Rex
Meaning of Name:	"Tyrant Lizard"
Scientific Name:	Velociraptor Mongoliensis
Dinosaur Type:	Tyrannosaur
Era on timeline:	Late Cretaceous Period
Fossils Found:	United States, Canada, Mongolia
Diet:	Carnivore
Hunting method:	Predator
Size:	40' long

The T-Rex had cone shaped teeth that were constantly replaced through its lifetime. Its mouth contained 50 to 60 teeth, some up to nine inches long.

Once thought to be a slow moving scavenger some scientists now think that T-Rexes were fast hunters propelled by powerful muscles that connected their legs to their tail.

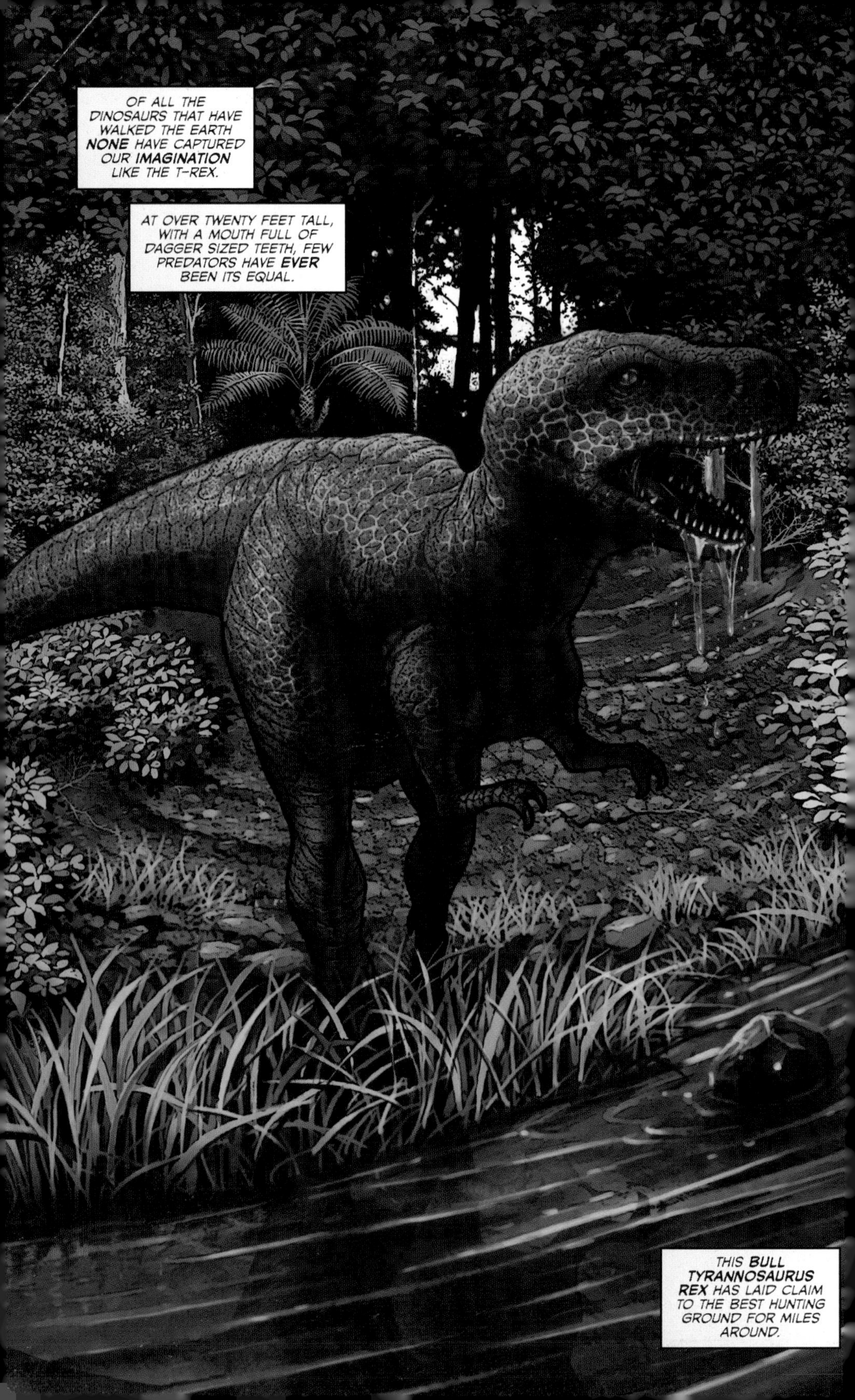
OF ALL THE DINOSAURS THAT HAVE WALKED THE EARTH **NONE** HAVE CAPTURED OUR **IMAGINATION** LIKE THE T-REX.
AT OVER TWENTY FEET TALL, WITH A MOUTH FULL OF DAGGER SIZED TEETH, FEW PREDATORS HAVE **EVER** BEEN ITS EQUAL.
THIS **BULL TYRANNOSAURUS REX** HAS LAID CLAIM TO THE BEST HUNTING GROUND FOR MILES AROUND.

FIERCELY **TERRITORIAL**, THE BULL WOULD NOT NORMALLY LET ANOTHER TYRANNOSAURUS INTO ITS TERRITORY.

BUT IT IS THE **MATING SEASON** AND FOR **ONCE** THE T-REX WELCOMES **ANOTHER** OF ITS SPECIES INTO ITS TERRITORY.

BUT **ONE** THING IS **NEVER** WELCOME IN THIS BULL'S TERRITORY...

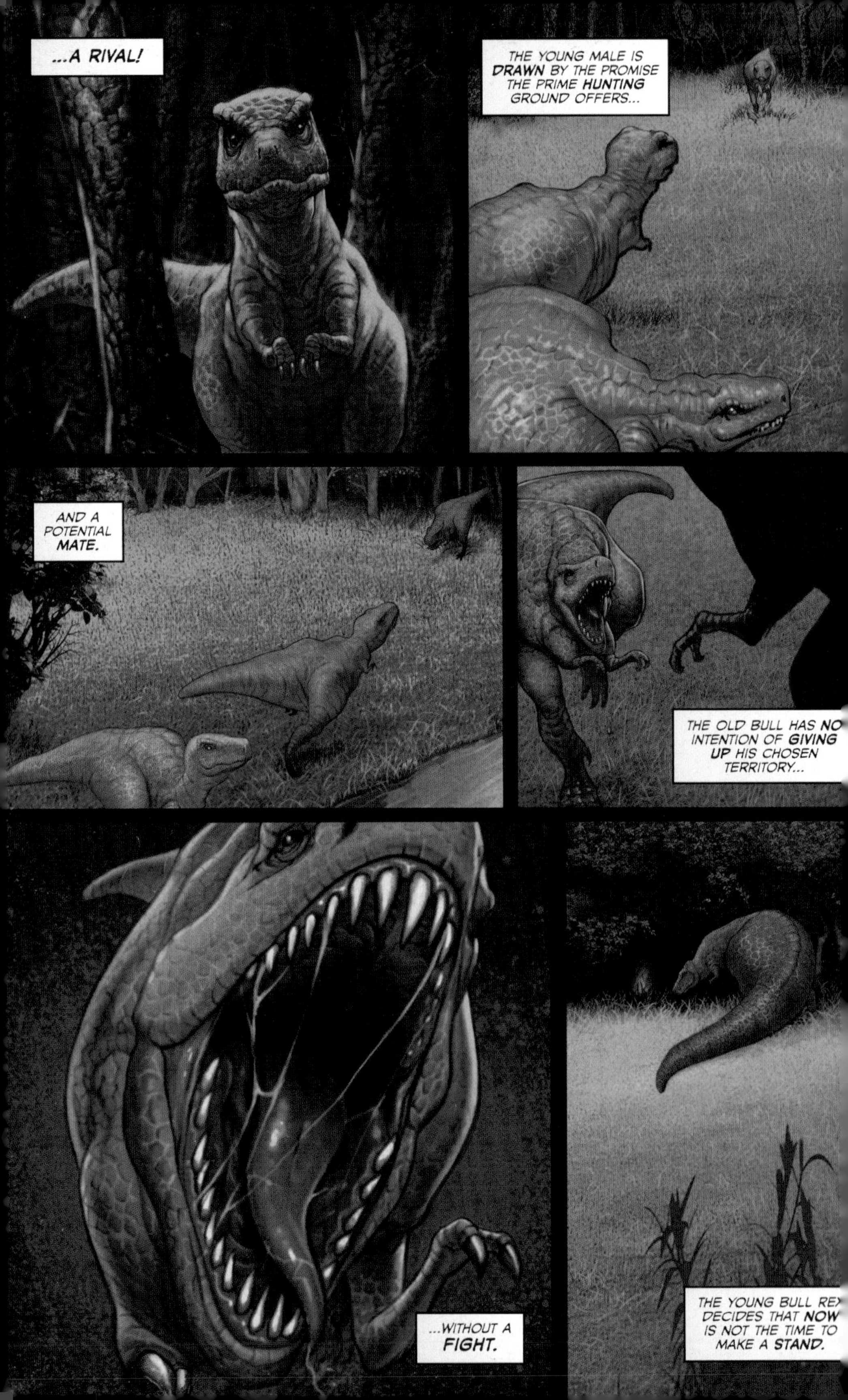
...A RIVAL!
THE YOUNG MALE IS DRAWN BY THE PROMISE THE PRIME HUNTING GROUND OFFERS...
AND A POTENTIAL MATE.
THE OLD BULL HAS NO INTENTION OF GIVING UP HIS CHOSEN TERRITORY...
...WITHOUT A FIGHT.
THE YOUNG BULL REX DECIDES THAT NOW IS NOT THE TIME TO MAKE A STAND.

OTHER DINOSAURS ALSO FREQUENT THE WATERING HOLE AND BEAR **WITNESS** TO THE DANCE TO COME.

HEY MUST RISK THE REAT OF AN **ATTACK** R A LIFE-SUSTAINING **DRINK.**

THE EXPERIENCED T-REX IS **CAUTIOUS.**

THWAK

IT'S WARY OF THE NKLYOSAUR'S NATURAL EAPONS, NOTABLY ITS POWERFUL **TAIL.**

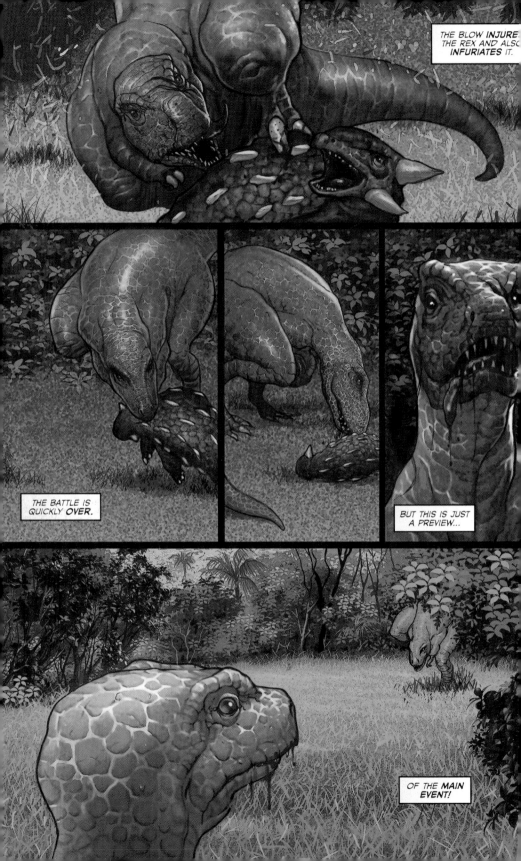

THE BLOW INJURE
THE REX AND ALSC
INFURIATES IT.

THE BATTLE IS
QUICKLY OVER.

BUT THIS IS JUST
A PREVIEW...

OF THE MAIN
EVENT!

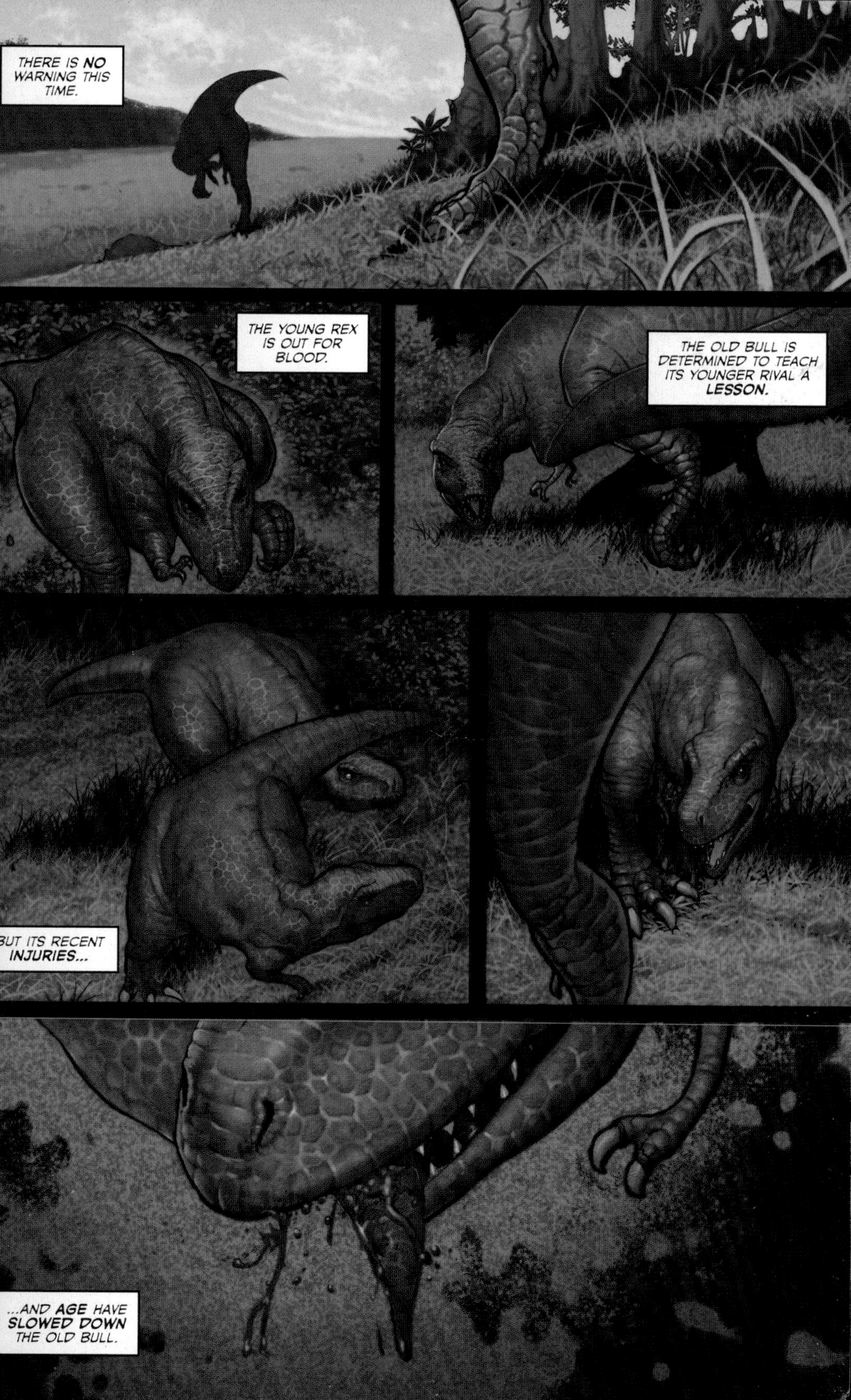

THERE IS NO WARNING THIS TIME.
THE YOUNG REX IS OUT FOR BLOOD.
THE OLD BULL IS DETERMINED TO TEACH ITS YOUNGER RIVAL A LESSON.
BUT ITS RECENT INJURIES...
...AND AGE HAVE SLOWED DOWN THE OLD BULL.

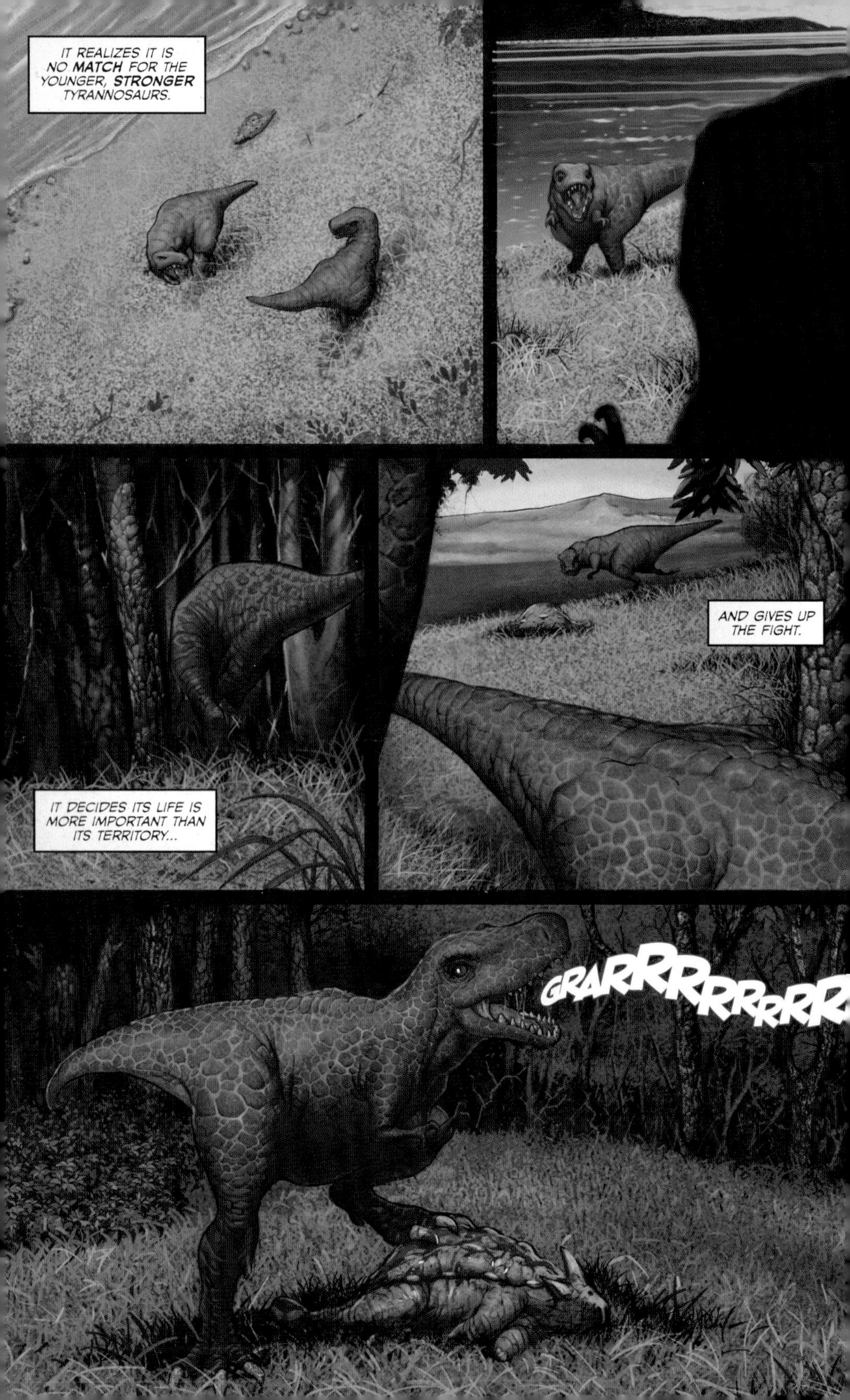
IT REALIZES IT IS NO MATCH FOR THE YOUNGER, STRONGER TYRANNOSAURS.
IT DECIDES ITS LIFE IS MORE IMPORTANT THAN ITS TERRITORY...
AND GIVES UP THE FIGHT.
GRARRRRRRRRR

WEAK AND INJURED, THE OLD TYRANNOSAUR LOOKS FOR AN **EASY MEAL.**

BUT IN THE WORLD OF THE DINOSAURS THOSE ARE NOT EASILY **FOUND.**

[I]F THE REX DOES NOT [RE]COVER AND REGAIN [TH]E **STRENGTH** TO HUNT [LI]VE PREY IT WILL SOON DIE.

[E]VEN IF IT **DOES** RECOVER, [A]GE AND THE LOSS OF ITS PRIME **HUNTING** GROUND MAY BE TOO **MUCH** FOR THE OLD BULL TO OVERCOME.

EVEN THE MOST FEROCIOUS TYRANNOSAURUS CANNOT DEFEAT THE **GREATEST** OF ALL ITS ENEMIES -- TIME.

THE **FIRST** T-REX FOSSIL WAS FOUND BY **BARNUM BROWN** IN 1902 IN HELL CREEK, MONTANA, USA, NORTH AMERICA.

ABOUT **THIRTY** INCOMPLETE T-REX FOSSILS HAVE BEEN FOUND TO DATE.

FACT FILE

Scientists believe the Tyrannosaurus Rex had superior sense of smell and sight, helping make the creature a powerful, deadly predator. It is also thought the beast walked leaning forward, balancing its head with its tail, which was held off the ground.

TRICERATOPS

Triceratops grew to as large as 30 feet long and 7 feet tall at the hips, and might have weighed as much as 12 tons.

The animal's head was the Triceratops' most distinctive feature. it could be almost one-third the length of its entire body and was crowned by a bony frill around its neck.

Triceratops' snout was topped by a relatively short horn, like that of the modern-day rhinoceros, with larger 3-foot long horns above each eye.

FACT FILE

Common Name:	Triceratops
Meaning of Name:	Three-horned face
Scientific Name:	Triceratops horridus
Dinosaur Type:	Ceratopsians
Era on Timeline:	Late Cretaceous Period
Fossils Found:	Western United States and Canada
Diet:	Herbivore
Hunting Method:	Grazer
Size:	30' long

LATE IN THE **CRETACEOUS** PERIOD, SOME 65 TO 72 MILLION YEARS AGO, NEAR THE **END** OF THE GREAT AGE OF DINOSAURS, NORTH AMERICA'S PREDOMINANT CITIZEN WAS THE MASSIVE **TRICERATOPS.**

THIS **FEARSOME** LOOKING GIANT WAS, IN REALITY, MOST LIKELY A PEACEFUL **HERBIVORE,** THRIVING ON THE FLORA THAT FLOURISHED ACROSS THE HOT, HUMID PLAINS.

TRICERATOPS WAS A MEMBER OF A GROUP OF **BEAKED HERBIVORES** THAT STRETCHED BACK TO THE **JURASSIC** PERIOD, AMONG THE **LARGEST** OF THE CERATOPSIA, OR "HORNED FACES"...

...BUT FOR ALL ITS **NUMBERS, SIZE,** AND **MONSTROUS APPEARANCE,** THE THREE-HORNED TRICERATOPS WAS **NOT** THE **MASTER** OF ITS WORLD.

NEAR THE **TOP OF THE** ALMOST *200 MILLION* YEARS OF EVOLUTIONARY ADAPTATION IN THE AGE OF DINOSAURS, WAS THE TYRANNOSAURUS REX...

...A FEROCIOUS 40-FOOT LONG, 13-TON **CARNIVORE** ARMED WITH POWERFUL JAW MUSCLES, AS WELL AS **SPEED** AND **MANEUVERABILITY.**

DANGER WAS ALWAYS LURKING IN THIS PREHISTORIC AGE AND, WHILE TRICERATOPS' **HORNS** WERE LIKELY USED FOR **DEFENSE...**

...MOST TIMES THE MIGHTY **TYRANT LIZARD** WOULD EMERGE THE VICTOR!

MOST HERBIVORES TRAVELED IN *HERDS*, BUT SINCE SO FEW *BONE BEDS* WITH THE REMAINS OF MORE THAN ONE ANIMAL HAVE BEEN FOUND, IT IS NOT *CERTAIN* TRICERATOPS WAS *ONE* OF THEM.

ANOTHER *MYSTERY* IS THE *LIFESPAN* OF TRICERATOPS. THEY HATCHED FROM EGGS LAID IN *SHALLOW HOLES* PACKED WITH MUD AND VEGETATION...

...AND THEIR FOSSIL REMAINS FROM *ALL* STAGES OF LIFE, FROM *HATCHLINGS* TO *ADULTS*, HAVE BEEN FOUND --

-- BUT IT IS IMPOSSIBLE TO TELL HOW *LONG* THEY MIGHT HAVE ACTUALLY *LIVED!*

THIS TRICERATOPS WOULD HAVE LIVED ON THE PREHISTORIC PRAIRIES, FEEDING ON THE ABUNDANT VEGETATION THAT GREW THERE.

THE JAWS OF HIS **MASSIVE HEAD** WERE FILLED WITH COLUMNS OF ANYWHERE FROM **400** TO **800** TEETH!

THE **HUNGRY** TRICERATOPS WOULD STRIP LEAVES, SEEDS, AND FLOWERS FROM PLANTS WITH HIS **POWERFUL BEAK.**

THESE TEETH WERE DESIGNED TO **SHEAR** AND **GRIND** A HUGE VOLUME OF A VARIETY OF VEGETATIONS, INCLUDING CYCADS, PALMS, FERNS, CONIFERS, AND FLOWERING PLANTS.

HE MIGHT EVEN HAVE USED HIS **HORNS** OR MASSIVE **SIZE** TO **KNOCK DOWN** TALLER PLANTS TO REACH THEIR EDIBLE TOPS.

TRICERATOPS MUST HAVE REQUIRED AN **TREMENDOUS** AMOUNT OF VEGETATION TO **SUSTAIN** HIS ENORMOUS SIZE.

HIS LIFE WAS LIKELY SPENT ON THE MOVE, IN **CONSTANT** SEARCH OF **FOOD.**

TRICERATOPS' MOST **STRIKING** FEATURES WERE THE **THREE HORNS** PROTRUDING FROM HIS GREAT, ARMORED HEAD...

...TOPPED WITH A SHORT BONY **FRILL** LIKE A **COLLAR.**

THERE ARE **SEVERAL** THEORIES OVER THE FUNCTION OF THESE **SCARY** APPENDAGES.

ONE IS THAT THEY WERE USED AMONG THEMSELVES AS A WAY OF **IDENTIFYING** EACH OTHER...

...AS WELL AS SERVING AS A DISPLAY IN **COURTSHIP.**

MANY EXPERTS ALSO BELIEVE THEY WERE THE TRICERATOPS' PRIMARY **DEFENSE** AGAINST PREDATORS.

BECAUSE OF HIS BULK AND SHORT LEGS, WITH A GAIT PROBABLY SIMILAR TO A THAT OF THE MODERN **RHINOCEROS**, TRICERATOPS WAS NOT **FAST** OR **AGILE**.

NOR WAS HIS BEAK, ADAPTED FOR GATHERING AND CHEWING VEGETATION, **STRONG** ENOUGH TO BE USED **DEFENSIVELY**.

FOSSIL EVIDENCE, INCLUDING TRICERATOPS BONES AND HORNS WITH TYRANNOSAURUS **TEETH-MARKS** ON THEM, PROVE THAT THE GREAT CARNIVORES **DID** FEED ON THE HORN-FACED GIANTS.

BUT T-REX **TEETH MARKS** ON BROKEN BROW HORN FOSSILS, THAT SHOW **NEW** BONE GROWTH **AFTER** THE BREAK...

...ALSO **PROVE** THAT NOT ONLY DID TRICERATOPS **FIGHT BACK** AGAINST THE LARGER ANIMAL --

-- BUT SOMETIMES, HE EVEN **SURVIVED** THE ENCOUNTER!

TRICERATOPS HAD NEITHER THE **SPEED** OR **STRENGTH** TO HAVE OFFENSIVELY **CHARGED** A LARGER PREDATOR...

...SO HE LIKELY **DEFENDED** HIMSELF BY HOLDING HIS GROUND AND USING HIS BROW HORNS TO **GORE** AND **WARD OFF** ATTACK.

THE BONY FRILL ON HIS HEAD ALSO **PROTECTED** TRICERATOPS' VULNERABLE **NECK.**

AT THE **END** OF THE CRETACEOUS PERIOD, EARTH WOULD UNDERGO A MASSIVE **EXTINCTION EVENT** THAT WOULD WIPE OUT VIRTUALLY **ALL** DINOSAUR SPECIES.

THE EVENT WAS MOST LIKELY TRIGGERED BY A LARGE **ASTEROID IMPACT** THAT COVERED THE PLANET IN A SHROUD OF **DUST** AND **SMOKE.**

BUT UNTIL THAT CATASTROPHE STRUCK THE TRICERATOPS LIVED AMONG THOSE AMAZING DINOSAURS THAT STILL CAPTURE OUR IMAGINATION TODAY ... 100 MILLION YEARS AFTER THEIR DEMISE.

FOR **MILLIONS** OF YEARS BEFORE THAT, THESE GREAT HORNED **GIANTS,** THE LAST OF THEIR KIND, WALKED THE EARTH... UNAWARE THAT THEIR TIME WAS ALMOST **OVER.**

VELOCIRAPTOR

Velociraptor had a deadly sickle shaped retractable claw on the middle toe of each foot.

FACT FILE

Common Name:	Velociraptor
Meaning of Name:	"Speedy Thief"
Scientific Name:	Velociraptor Mongoliensis
Dinosaur Type:	Dromaeosaurids
Era on Timeline:	Late Cretaeceous Period
Fossils Found:	China, Mongolia and Russia
Diet:	Carnivore
Hunting Method:	Pack Hunter
Size:	6' long

The Velociraptor's tail, curved sideways into an S-shape. This helped the Velociraptor to be stable, while turning at a high speed.

The Raptors clawed hands were its most effective hunting weapon.

80 MILLION YEARS AGO A PREDATOR NOT MUCH LARGER THAN OUR MODERN DAY *LION* TERRORIZED THE FORESTS AND PLAINS OF THE LATE CRETACEOUS PERIOD.

THE VELOCIRAPTOR WAS ARMED WITH A MORE IMPRESSIVE ARRAY OF *WEAPONS* THAN A LION, OR ANY *OTHER* PREDATOR THAT WALKS THE EARTH TODAY.

MANY PALEONTOLOGISTS BELIEVE THAT *VELOCIRAPTORS* WERE *PACK* ANIMALS.

EVIDENCE TO BACK THAT THEORY UP HAS BEEN DISCOVERED IN VELOCIRAPTOR **FOSSILS.**

THROUGH THAT FOSSIL EVIDENCE WE CAN THEORIZE **HOW** PACKS OF RAPTORS **LIVED.**

IN ANIMAL PACKS THERE IS ALWAYS A **PECKING ORDER.**

YOUNG ADULT ANIMALS ARE OFTEN CHARGED WITH THE CARE AND **PROTECTION** OF THE PACK'S **YOUNGEST** MEMBERS.

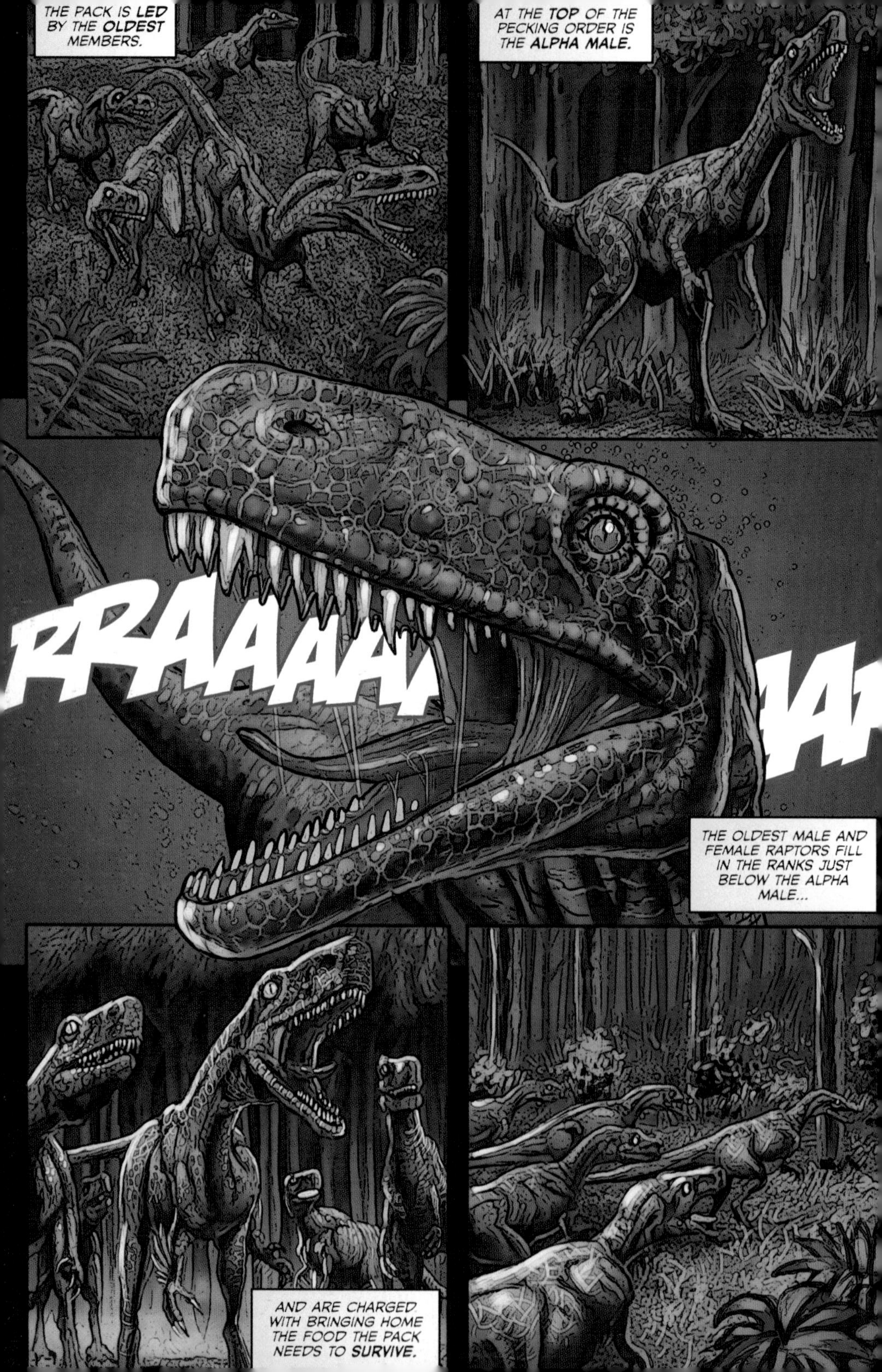
THE PACK IS LED BY THE OLDEST MEMBERS.
AT THE TOP OF THE PECKING ORDER IS THE ALPHA MALE.
RRAAAAAAAAR
THE OLDEST MALE AND FEMALE RAPTORS FILL IN THE RANKS JUST BELOW THE ALPHA MALE...
AND ARE CHARGED WITH BRINGING HOME THE FOOD THE PACK NEEDS TO SURVIVE.

THE PACK MOVES AS ONE IN SEARCH OF PREY.

ALONE THEY ARE DANGEROUS.

TOGETHER THEY FORM AN UNSTOPPABLE HUNTING TEAM.

THEY HEAD TOWARDS THEIR FAVORITE HUNTING GROUNDS.

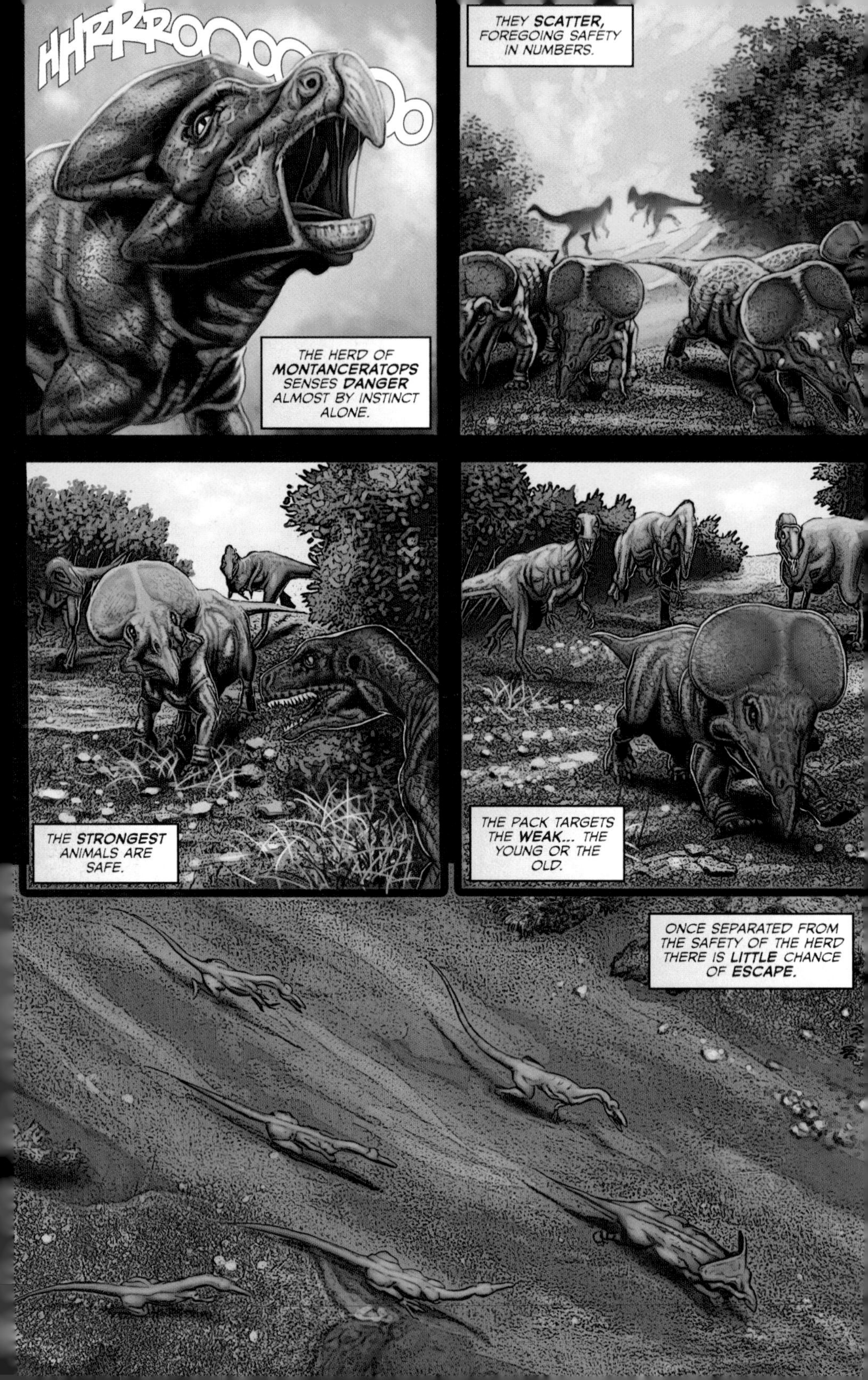
HHRRROOOOOOO
THE HERD OF MONTANCERATOPS SENSES DANGER ALMOST BY INSTINCT ALONE.
THEY SCATTER, FOREGOING SAFETY IN NUMBERS.
THE STRONGEST ANIMALS ARE SAFE.
THE PACK TARGETS THE WEAK... THE YOUNG OR THE OLD.
ONCE SEPARATED FROM THE SAFETY OF THE HERD THERE IS LITTLE CHANCE OF ESCAPE.

THE **ALPHA MALE** IS GIVEN THE HONOR OF THE **KILL**.

SHRRIP

THE REST OF THE PACK AWAITS ITS **TURN** THEN TAKE THEIR **SHARE**.

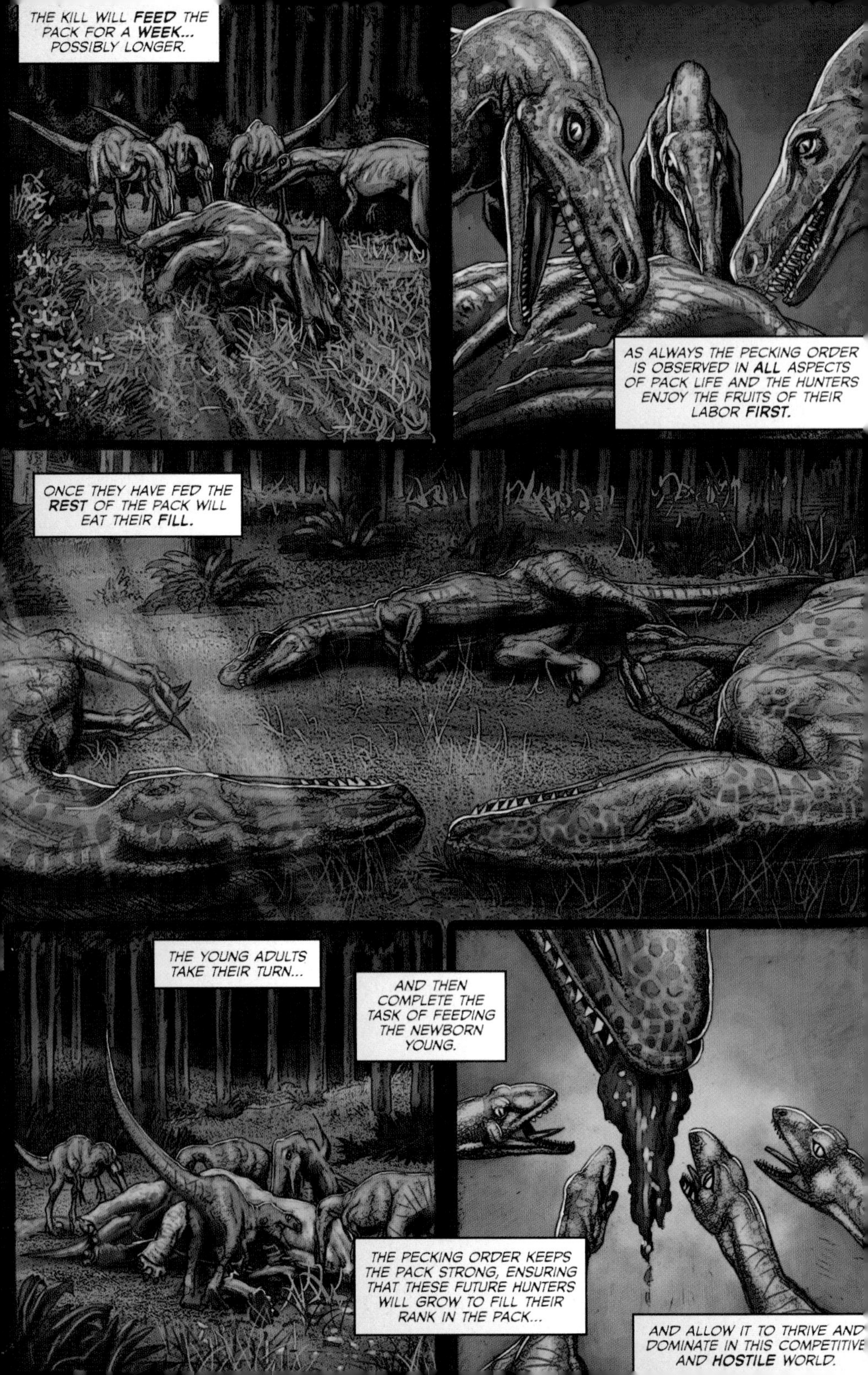
THE KILL WILL FEED THE PACK FOR A WEEK... POSSIBLY LONGER.
AS ALWAYS THE PECKING ORDER IS OBSERVED IN ALL ASPECTS OF PACK LIFE AND THE HUNTERS ENJOY THE FRUITS OF THEIR LABOR FIRST.
ONCE THEY HAVE FED THE REST OF THE PACK WILL EAT THEIR FILL.
THE YOUNG ADULTS TAKE THEIR TURN...
AND THEN COMPLETE THE TASK OF FEEDING THE NEWBORN YOUNG.
THE PECKING ORDER KEEPS THE PACK STRONG, ENSURING THAT THESE FUTURE HUNTERS WILL GROW TO FILL THEIR RANK IN THE PACK...
AND ALLOW IT TO THRIVE AND DOMINATE IN THIS COMPETITIVE AND HOSTILE WORLD.

FACT FILE

There is still much debate among scientists about what Velociraptors and many dinosaurs really looked like. Some scientists think they are the ancestors of our modern day birds and that they were been covered with feathers, giving them the appearance of large flightless predators.

THE DISCOVERY CONTINUES...

EVERY YEAR, **NEW DISCOVERIES** ARE MADE THAT TEACH US MORE ABOUT HOW THE MIGHTY DINOSAURS LIVED. IN UTAH ALONE, THERE WERE **EIGHT NEW SPECIES** NAMED IN 2010, THE OLDEST DATING BACK 125 MILLION YEARS.

ALSO IN 2010, IN SOUTHWEST FRANCE, FRAGMENTS OF A **35-TON** HERBIVORE WERE UNEARTHED IN A QUARRY -- THE **LARGEST** DISCOVERED IN EUROPE.

THE FEMUR, MEASURING NEARLY **EIGHT FEET**, DATES FROM THE EARLY CRETACEOUS PERIOD, WHICH SCIENTISTS KNOW RELATIVELY LITTLE ABOUT.

UNFORTUNATELY THE RESOURCES AND EXPERTS AVAILABLE TO STUDY THE VAST AMOUNT OF DATA UNCOVERED IS **LIMITED**.

THIS CREATURE WAS PART OF THE **CARCHARODONTOSAURUS** -- A **GIGANTIC** CARNIVORE WITH SHARP TEETH, LARGER THAN THE TYRANNOSAURUS REX.

AS A RESULT THE PROCESS OF CONTINUING T BUILD ON OUR DATA BASE OF KNOWLEDGE ABOUT DINOSAURS IS SLOW GOING.

RESEARCHERS CARRY ON, THOUGH, AND WE CONTINUE TO REVISE OUR BELIEFS IN HOW MANY OF THESE MAGNIFICENT CREATURES LIVED.

IT WAS THEORIZED THAT 90 SPECIES OF THEROPODS FROM THE LATE TRIASSIC PERIOD ATE A PLANT-BASED DIET. MANY OF THE SPECIES ARE THOUGHT TO HAVE EVOLVED THROUGH THE CENTURIES TO BECOME THE BIRDS WE KNOW TODAY.

IN 2010, THE NATIONAL ACADEMY OF SCIENCES ANNOUNCED THEIR BELIEF THAT MOST OF THE GIANT, FEROCIOUS CREATURES WERE ACTUAL VEGETARIANS.

DISCOVERIES AROUND THE GLOBE CONTINUE TO REFINE OUR UNDERSTANDING OF THEIR LIVES, AN UNENDING EDUCATION AS WE DISCOVER NEW FOSSILS AND EVIDENCE.

THE DINOSAURS, ONCE THE WORLD'S MIGHTY RULERS, CONTINUE TO CAPTURE OUR IMAGINATIONS AS WE TRY AND ENVISION WHAT THEIR LIVES MIGHT HAVE BEEN LIKE, AND HOW OUR WORLD LOOKED LONG BEFORE MAN WALKED THE LAND.

CAIO CACAU

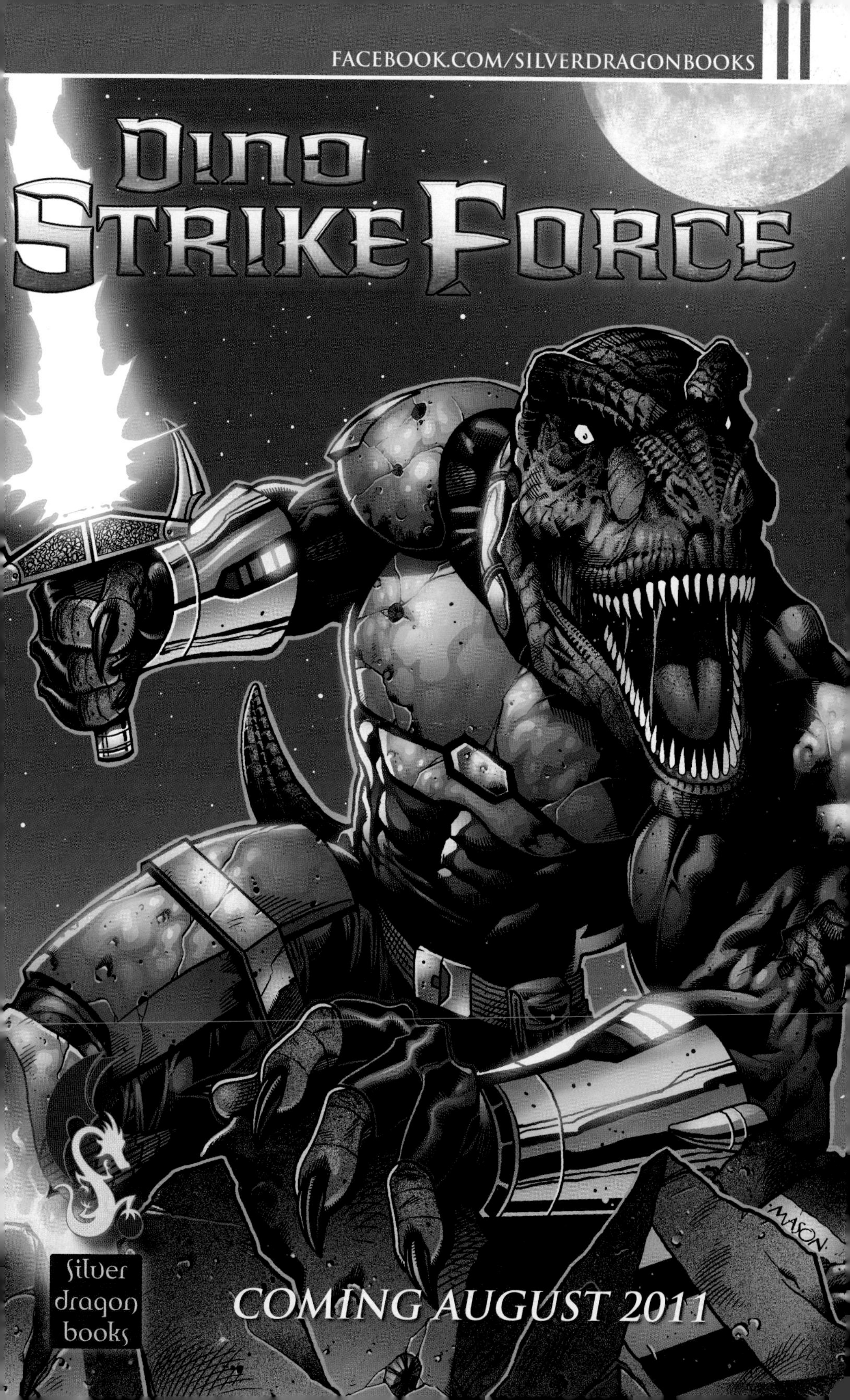
FACEBOOK.COM/SILVERDRAGONBOOKS
DINO STRIKE FORCE
MASON
silver dragon books
COMING AUGUST 2011

TOP 10
DEADLIEST
SHARKS

IN STORES NOW